Who do you say you are?

finding your *true self* in chronic illness

Published by **Redemptorist Publications**
Alphonsus House, Chawton, Hampshire, GU34 3HQ, UK

Tel. +44 (0)1420 88222, Fax. +44 (0)1420 88805
Email rp@rpbooks.co.uk, www.rpbooks.co.uk

A registered charity limited by guarantee
Registered in England 3261721

Copyright © Redemptorist Publications 2017
First published July 2017

Text by Lucy Russell
Edited by Therese Garman
Designed by Christine Reissland & Eliana Thompson

ISBN 978-0-85231-483-8

A CIP catalogue record for this book is available from the British Library.

Excerpts from the New Revised Standard Version of the Bible: Anglicised Edition, © 1989. 1995, Division of Christian Education of the National Council of the Churches of Christ in the United States of America. Used by permission. All rights reserved.

Every effort has been made to trace copyright holders and to obtain their permission for the use of copyright material. The publisher apologises for any errors or omissions and would be grateful for notification of any corrections that should be incorporated in future reprints or editions of this book.

Printed and bound by John Dollin Printing Services Ltd, Whitchurch, Hants, RG28 7BB

Who do you say you are?

finding your true self
in chronic illness

Lucy Russell

redemptorist
p u b l i c a t i o n s

This book is for Sheila, and for Fr Duncan Lourensz.
I couldn't have done it without you both, or without the
love and support of my family and my friends
Alison, Kate, and especially Phil.
Thank you.

My Lord God, I have no idea where I am going.

I do not see the road ahead of me.

I cannot know for certain where it will end.

Nor do I really know myself, and the fact that I think that I am following your will does not mean that I am actually doing so.

But I believe that the desire to please you does in fact please you. And I hope I have that desire in all that I am doing. I hope that I will never do anything apart from that desire. And I know that if I do this you will lead me by the right road, though I may know nothing about it.

Therefore I will trust you always, though I may seem to be lost and in the shadow of death. I will not fear, for you are ever with me, and you will never leave me to face my perils alone.

A Prayer from *Thoughts in Solitude*
by Thomas Merton (1956)

God knows
who I am

Contents

"Hope" is an important word.

My Soul Praises the Lord

For thirteen years, I said I wouldn't write about my Multiple Sclerosis. With the exception of those closest to me, and the people who needed to know, I didn't even tell anyone about it. I never expected to write a book that discussed my MS. But that changed when I met Sheila. She had agreed to meet me to talk about her work at the local Foodbank for an article I had been asked to write. Our conversation became quite wide ranging, and I suddenly blurted out that I had a diagnosis of MS. A revelation, I quickly followed with, "I'm sorry, I don't know why I just told you that. I don't normally talk about it." Sheila smiled, "perhaps you needed to tell someone."

This book isn't about MS, or living with a chronic condition. It is about what makes us who we are. I told Sheila that my MS was something I treated with the contempt it deserved, and ignored it in the hope that it would not get any worse. "Hope" is an important word. So far, I have been lucky with my MS. It was a difficult time when it was diagnosed, but I felt hopeful that it might not get worse and I should be able to live reasonably normally with the condition. I was also relieved that I didn't have an even worse neurological condition or a brain tumour. Sheila's reaction to my "treat it with contempt" surprised me. "You shouldn't treat it with contempt," she said gently. "It's a part of you, to be embraced." Her words struck me, and put me in mind of Mo Mowlam, and a scene from Neil McKay's 2010 biopic, Mo.

Towards the end of the film, Mo's doctor pays her a visit and explains that her brain tumour was there long before she even noticed any of the symptoms it caused. She could have had the tumour for more than twenty years. Mo asks her doctor if the symptoms, the disinhibition and personality change, could go back twenty years. "Yes," says her doctor. Mo replies, "So, good old Mo, the Mo that everybody loves, larger-than-life Mo, that could all be because of the tumour?" Mo wonders what part of her personality is really her, and what part is the tumour. That resonated with me. I had never thought of my MS as part of me. Had I spent thirteen years denying a part of myself? Had I really spent all that time trying to prove I was someone else? I began to think that I had.

Looking back, it is easy to see how that happened. I didn't want to give in to my MS and let it define me. So I hid it. This was partly about control, and me maintaining that. There were other reasons too. I wanted to protect the people closest to me from any anxiety about me. There was also a question about how others might perceive me and my MS, which I didn't want to be held against me in social or professional situations. Delta Goodrem sings about not being the girl she once was in her song, *Mistaken Identity*:

"The girl I used to be has a terrible case of mistaken identity
And yesterday's girl is not what you see."

Billy Mann and Delta Goodrem,
Mistaken Identity (2004)

I wanted to be the girl that I was. I wanted people to see me, not my condition.

When I had my younger son, I met a Health Visitor who asked me if I would be interested in attending a support group for people living with MS. She told me – in confidence – that she also had MS and was thinking about setting up such a group. At that point in time, I wanted to ignore my MS and pretend it wasn't there. What was interesting about our conversation, was her concern that I didn't tell anybody what she had revealed to me. Her colleagues didn't know. I wonder how many people we are all living alongside are concealing a condition? No-one should have to divulge their medical state to anybody. I wasn't ready to share my secret openly until I met Sheila, but since becoming more open about my MS, I have received more support when I have needed it. I'm matter-of-fact about who I am, and model how I want to be treated. And as a result there is actually less fuss, because people understand and ignore, or work around, the times when I look tired, or seem slightly incoherent, or have lost my grip and dropped something. Only God is perfect, we are not, and we don't have to be. Events and experiences – good and bad - change and shape us, and I stopped being the girl I was when I became unwell and went through the process of being diagnosed with MS. Kathryn Greene-McCreight writes something quite beautiful in her book *I Am With You*: "The people of God is not just a collection of individuals, but a web of relationships created by God. We are not our own. We are not on our own" (Kathryn Greene-McCreight, *I Am With You* (London: Bloomsbury, 2015), 97-98. This is something that my MS has really brought home to me. It is how it has helped to shape me and make me who I am.

Having said that my MS has changed me, I have also remained the same. Like Mo's brain tumour, my MS was there before it was diagnosed. In a poem written shortly before his death, Dietrich Bonhoeffer asked, "Am I one person today and tomorrow another?" This is a poignant question for those facing illnesses which affect memory and personality. How interesting that though the Archbishop of Canterbury, Justin Welby, has said that the news that his real father is Anthony Montague-Brown, came as a "complete surprise", he has said, "There is no existential crisis, and no resentment against anyone. My identity is founded in who I am in Christ" ("Justin Welby's personal story of courage is better than a thousand sermons," *The Telegraph*, 8 April 2016). It is in recognising Christ that we understand who we are. Look at Peter's profession of faith in Matthew's Gospel: "Who do you say that I am?" Jesus asks his disciples. "You are the Messiah" responds Peter, "the Son of the living God." Jesus replies, "And I say to you: You are Peter and on this rock I will build my Church" (Matthew 16:15-19). Peter recognises Christ, and Christ's immediate response is to tell Peter who he is.

I have spent some time reflecting on Sheila's words to me. In one way, they were a relief. If I accept my MS as a part of myself and who I am, then I don't have to fight it any more, or drive myself quite so hard to try to prove I am in charge of it, rather than the other way around. I sometimes think about other opportunities I might have taken had it not been for the MS, and how life may have been different. But this is how it is (and perhaps how it was meant to be). I am not the girl I thought I was. I don't take anything for granted. I take every opportunity that comes my way, and appreciate all the small things: the wind in the trees, the warmth of the sun, birdsong.

Delta's song is not the only one which resonates with me. While I was pulling together my notes for this book, I realised just how much of the music I like to listen to expresses thoughts about identity and what makes us who we are. Throughout this book I have drawn on this music, which has brought a knowing smile to my lips when I have heard the lyrics, or which I have sung along with, or cried through.

The chapter headings are inspired by Mary's song of praise. This song is deeply moving and inspiring. God has a plan for Mary, which she doesn't understand, yet which she not only chooses to accept, but for which she also offers a hymn of praise. Can I reflect her courage and trust? There is more about Mary's song in Chapter Six. I don't know what I came here for. None of us knows what we are here for. What we do know is that all are equally important in God's eyes, and bring joy to God. For those of us in a position to make a positive difference, the question is how we make our lives count. A better understanding of who we are and what our role might be, is the subject of Chapter Two.

It has been scientifically proven that singing is good for us, body and soul. I have juxtaposed the spiritual and meditative with contemporary music throughout. Each chapter begins with a few verses from one of the psalms which are particularly relevant to that chapter. These sacred songs about Israel's hopes and fears, triumphs and disasters, loves and hates, are telling. We are still singing about the same things. In this book I have talked about music that resonates with me, there will be other pop songs and pieces of music which resonate with you and which tell your story. This book is my story of the process of my diagnosis and my coming to terms with that and finding myself within it, told against a backdrop of sacred and contemporary song. The point here is that the world might change, music might change, but human beings are the same. And so is God.

Lord, you have been our dwelling place in all generations.
Before the mountains were brought forth,
or ever you had formed the earth and the world,
from everlasting to everlasting you are God.

PSALM 90:1-2

...being loved and accepted as you are

Chapter One

My Spirit Rejoices in God

O Lord, you have searched me and known me.

You know when I sit down and when I rise up; you discern my thoughts from far away.

You search out my path and my lying down, and are acquainted with all my ways.

Even before a word is on my tongue, O Lord, you know it completely.

You hem me in, behind and before, and lay your hand upon me.

Such knowledge is too wonderful for me; it is so high that I cannot attain it.

For it was you who formed my inward parts; you who knit me together in my mother's womb.

I praise you, for I am fearfully and wonderfully made.

Wonderful are your works; that I know very well.

My frame was not hidden from you, when I was being made in secret, Intricately woven in the depths of the earth.

Your eyes beheld my unformed substance.

In your book were written all the days that were formed for me, when none of them as yet existed.

How weighty to me are your thoughts, O God!

How vast is the sum of them!

I try to count them – they are more than the sand;

I come to the end – I am still with you.

PSALM 139:1-6, 13-18

O Lord, you have searched me and known me

PSALM 139:1

I was originally thinking of using song titles as chapter headings, and perhaps using Meredith Brooks' song *Bitch*, or the first line from this track, as the heading for this chapter. The song was co-written with Shelly Peiken. It's a track that I have always loved. Psychotherapist Julia Samuel chose it as one of her *Desert Island Discs*, when she took part in the BBC Radio 4 Programme. Julia told presenter Kirsty Young that she felt the track had a certain "punch" to it that she really liked, and dedicated the song to her "best girlfriends who know me really well, and love me whatever I am like" (*Desert Island Discs*, BBC Radio 4, 6 March 2015). That is exactly what this song is about: being loved and accepted as you are. What I find particularly noteworthy is the chorus, which highlights all the different people we are, the multiple identities we each have. As it says in the chorus of Meredith's song, I am a child, a mother, a sinner and a saint. It is a fabulous track, whose stark lyrics I am happy to sing along with, loudly, as I clear the kitchen table, and before I put on some music from *Taizé* and get ready to start writing. As Meredith sings, we are all, "a little bit of everything, all rolled into one"; which is obvious really, since we are made in the image and likeness of God, and God is everything in one.

I know you are near is one of my favourite hymns, and is based on Psalm 139. It didn't surprise me to learn that this was written by Daniel Schutte, who is perhaps best known for composing *Here I Am, Lord*, which was one of the hymns at my wedding. The first six verses from Psalm 139 remind me that God knows exactly what makes each of us who we are, and holds all our different identities. These verses also put me in mind of another lifechanging experience: becoming a mother. When I held my eldest child for the first time, such was the sense of awe and wonder I experienced, that I forced myself to think of something other than God and creation. I told myself to try and put off exploring the thoughts in my mind until I wasn't so tired. I have never been more aware of God's presence. It seemed as though suddenly everything made sense. I suddenly understood, but that understanding was too great to contemplate. James was a miracle, and gave meaning to my life. As a writer my instinct was to try and put my thoughts into words, but I didn't have the words. I was so overwhelmed I effectively turned my back on God, pushing these thoughts out of my mind until a later time when I thought I would feel able to cope with and contemplate them. But that time never came. Looking back, I see those thoughts not as something to be explored and organised, but as a complete experience which transcended words. Just as it is written in Psalm 139: the knowledge was too wonderful and I couldn't attain it.

St Augustine wrote, "People travel to wonder at the heights of mountains, at the huge waves of the seas, at the long course of the rivers, at the vast compass of the ocean, at the circular motions of the stars, and yet they pass by themselves without wondering." Before I sat down to write this Chapter, I'm not sure I had ever given all that much thought to who I understood myself to be. Julia Samuel told Kirsty Young that, "Having greater insight into yourself and a greater awareness of all the different aspects of what you are feeling, of what is happening in you, gives you more choices." She went on to say that when we feel more connected to ourselves, that allows us to be more connected to other people, "And when you have that, you feel that you have more resilience and more efficacy in the world" (*Desert Island Discs*, BBC Radio 4, 6 March 2015).

Our sense of identity is perhaps the most important influence which determines our actions. We act according to our view of who we really are. Stephen Covey, author of *The 7 Habits of Highly Effective People: Powerful Lessons in Personal Change* (Free Press, 1989), says, "We are not in control, principles control. We control our actions, but the consequences that flow from these actions are controlled by principles." Our principles and values are part of our identity. Who am I in essence? I have spent some time thinking about that question.

I praise you, for I am fearfully and wonderfully made

PSALM 139:14A

My identity is certainly bound up with my faith. My friend's mother has a brain tumour. It's terminal, and there is very little that can be done except for creating good memories as a family and spending as much time together as possible. My friend leads a busy life. She teaches English at a secondary school three days a week, and she and her husband have two children, aged nine and five. Somehow, she is managing to travel 120 miles to her parent's house every other Wednesday to spend two and a half days supporting her father and helping with her mother's care. During an odd lunchtime when we manage to meet and catch up for the first time in four months, the busy-ness and the needs of others are temporarily put to one side, and it dawns on her what she is losing. "This," she confides in me, "is where some faith would be helpful".

I find my faith helpful. I can't separate this from who I am. A few years ago I heard Paschal Uche give a talk about his experience of the 2010 Papal visit to the UK. Paschal said it felt easy to be a Catholic in Britain at that time. Crowds of people welcomed Pope Benedict XVI. Being a Catholic is easy in the good times, having faith is easy in the good times. But what about in more challenging times? There can be a temptation to lead a double life and keep our Catholicism quiet. Pope Francis has warned against being a "lukewarm" Catholic, and has talked about the importance of safeguarding our Christian identity. We can all do that, starting with our own families and friends, by making our faith visible through the way we live our daily lives and arousing curiosity in Jesus. But there is a school of thought which says that religion should be kept separate from our daily lives and what we do, and that God should not be involved in issues of state. Former Downing Street spin doctor, Alastair Campbell, apparently said, "We don't do God" when the then Prime Minister, Tony Blair, was asked about his faith. But surely it is impossible to keep our faith separate from other areas of our lives, because it is who we are: "The Christian who doesn't necessarily want to cancel out his identity, but to dull it down (is the) lukewarm Christian," Pope Francis has said. "He is Christian, yes, he goes to Mass on Sunday, yes...He also lives like a pagan, but he is Christian. Being lukewarm. Dulling down our identity." These were comments made by the Pope during his homily at Mass on 17 October 2014, but he has spoken on the same theme of the dulling down of our Christian identity and the sin of hypocrisy on several other occasions. He's right. I would be a hypocrite if I went to church on a Sunday, listened to the Gospel and to my Parish Priest reflecting on how this could inform our daily lives, and then went home and didn't try to put those thoughts into action during the rest of the week. Surely faith has to be a publicly acknowledged commitment. As Tony Benn once said in an interview with Mary Kenny, "How can you separate yourself from the world you live in? I can't imagine a world where people have their religion in a water-tight compartment. Religion can't just be a private matter" (Mary Kenny, "Tony Benn 1925–2014: a politician shaped by

Christianity", *The Catholic Herald* (14 March 2014). Our faith impacts our actions. In ITV's 2010 television production of *Murder on the Orient Express* starring David Suchet, Hercule Poirot is seen praying with his Rosary beads: "...if I have done any good, deign to accept it." That's my kind of Catholicism. I hope that when I smile at someone in the street, or give someone a lift in the car, I am doing some good, and that God might deign to accept it.

Having faith doesn't mean that I don't experience doubt. Frank Skinner, speaking in September 2011 in conversation with the then Archbishop of Canterbury, Dr Rowan Williams, said:

Most of my conversations are with atheists, who say how can anyone with any kind of brain believe in God in 2011? How can you be so sure? And my point is, I'm not sure and in fact I think faith, that kind of complete and utter blind faith, is a very dangerous thing.

ARCHBISHOP ROWAN AND FRANK SKINNER
IN CONVERSATION (16 SEPTEMBER 2011)

Frank sees himself as a person of doubt, and says that doubt is an important part of being human. I think Frank's right. So when my friend asked me, over a glass of wine one day, "What if you're wrong?", I wasn't fazed. I might be wrong. But what if I'm not? And actually, what have any of us got to lose anyway? French philosopher, mathematician and physicist, Blaise Pascal (1623-1662), argued that given the possibility that God actually does exist, and assuming the infinite gain or loss associated with belief or unbelief in God, a rational person should live as though God exists. Pascal's wager is that you have more to gain than you have to lose by believing in God. But if you haven't been brought up with a belief in God, it can be hard to make that leap of faith. There is comfort to be derived from faith, and I am in an enviable position from my friend's perspective. There is part of her that would like to believe in God, but she doesn't feel she can make that leap. But as Blaise Pascal wrote, "Something incomprehensible is not for that reason less real."

The Austrian philosopher Ludwig Wittgenstein said, "To believe in a God means to realise that the facts of the world are not the whole story. To believe in a God means to realise that life has a meaning." This makes sense to me. God is where I find meaning. As C S Lewis put it, "I believe in Christianity as I believe that the sun has risen: not only because I see it, but because by it I see everything else." Catholic teaching says that we were made by Love for love. Faith, like falling in love, is a leap in the dark. Imagine being Mary Magdalene, discovering Jesus' empty tomb on Easter morning. Jesus hasn't been taken anywhere, but it will take a leap of faith for his closest friends to begin to accept this new reality. Mary asks, "Where have they taken my Lord?", but perhaps she might have more accurately asked, "Where are you taking me, Lord?" Faith is a journey. It's an adventure. That first appearance to Mary is the beginning of a journey of faith. Like that first appearance, there are times on our own journey of faith, when we are confronted with more questions than there are obvious answers. Mary Magdalene's pain is not taken away. This is a meeting that offers just enough comfort. Mary gets to spend a few minutes with her friend, and is reassured that what she thought was the end, is not. She doesn't get answers; there is no explanation. Mary probably doesn't understand what it all means as she leaves Jesus to tell the others the news. What she is given is hope.

Wonderful are your works; that I know very well

PSALM 139:14B

Key to my identity is my Catholicism, this is part of my being. My great-great-great-grandfather, William Wallace, was received into the Catholic Church on 12 February 1857, at the age of thirty. He had met Blessed Dominic Barberi in Sutton in Merseyside in 1849. Fr Dominic, who was Italian, was in Sutton to make preparations to build a new church, and William, who was a local resident, had been asked to go along because he spoke some Italian and it was thought he might be able to help with the negotiations. When Fr Dominic heard that William was not a Catholic, he looked at him earnestly and said, "I will pray for you: you will become a Catholic." Catholicism is part of my genealogy. Our genealogy pinpoints us, and tells us something about where we have come from. St Matthew begins his Gospel with the genealogy of Jesus. Where we have come from is important, but it isn't who we are. For me, the first chapter of St John's Gospel is far more powerful and beautiful than Matthew's. John begins his Gospel by saying that Jesus is the Son of God. And even more than that:

But to all who received him [Jesus], who believed in his name, he gave the power to become children of God, who were born, not of blood or the will of the flesh or of the will of man, but of God.

JOHN 1:12-13

Now, how incredibly wonderful is that? Wherever we have come from, whatever has happened, it is within ourselves and our power to become God's children. We find our significance in our relationship with God. I have proudly remained a part of the Catholic Church because of what the Church says about peace; justice; human dignity; equality; care for the environment; the importance of a good work life balance; and solidarity. When I went to Northern Ireland for a friend's wedding in 2002, I wondered whether I would be viewed first as Catholic or English. But whatever the answer is, I know in my heart, I am a Catholic before I am English. I like the subversive nature of that, and the fact that I am no more and no less important or worthy than anyone else. We are all equally loved. The Catholic Church protects and promotes life, and values everybody. Human dignity is something that can't be taken away. Catholic social teaching says that each and every person has value, is worthy of respect, and must be free from slavery, manipulation and exploitation. Pope Francis has written, "How can it be that it is not a news item when an elderly homeless person dies of exposure, but it is news when the stock market loses two points?" (Pope Francis, *Evangelii Gaudium* ("The Joy of the Gospel"), 53. It's a very good question. Cardinal Basil Hume, leader of the Catholic Church in England and Wales from 1976 until his death in 1999, said that "working for peace and justice is the central mission of the Church". The Catholic Church's vision is of a world where people can live in peace, without violence in any form. Pax Christi (which is Latin for the Peace of Christ) is an International Catholic Movement for Peace. Their work is rooted in Catholic Christianity and is based on what Jesus taught, but you don't have to be a Catholic to be involved with the organisation, it is open to anyone who shares its values and work. Pax Christi works for peace based on justice in a world where human rights are respected, basic needs are met, and people feel safe and valued in their communities. The Movement also promotes reconciliation and nonviolence.

It is commonly understood that Catholic social teaching developed as a response to the economic problems of the nineteenth century. Industrialisation led to an increase in prosperity, but those who profited from it were mainly factory owners, many sank into poverty as labourers with almost no rights. As a result, Communism drew the conclusion that there was an irreconcilable opposition between *labour* and *capital*, which must be decided by class war. But the Catholic Church, in contrast, argued for a fair balance between the interests of the labourers and those of the factory owners. The Church recommended that not only a few, but *everyone* should benefit from the prosperity that industrialisation and increasing competition brought. So, the Catholic Church supported the development of trade unions and advocated protecting labourers from exploitation through legislation and government assurances and insuring them and their families against sickness and emergencies. The Church is concerned about the well-being and just treatment of everyone, not just Christians. It is guided by a love that emulates Christ's love for humankind. I haven't made this up. It's all in the "rule book" – have a look at paragraphs 2419-2420 and 2422-2423 of the *Catechism of the Catholic Church*. The Catholic Church is motivated by love. Jesus gives just one commandment: love one another as I have loved you (John 13:34-35). That's it. Treat everyone the way you would like to be treated.

The word "religion" actually comes from the Latin word *religare* which means to bind or connect. What my Catholicism offers me is a bond with others, which helps to connect me to the wider world. That sense of togetherness, belonging and being a part of something, is important. As humans we need to belong. Any psychologist will tell you that a sense of belonging is fundamental to our happiness and well-being. Our interests, motivation, health and happiness are all tied in to our sense of belonging. Feelings of isolation and loneliness can harm our sense of well-being, which has an impact on intellectual achievement, immune function and health. There are times when we all need a bit of togetherness. Together we can make a difference, together we are stronger. You often find a strong sense of community in parish churches, where people come together old and young. There aren't many other places where that happens. The word Catholic actually comes from the Latin *catholicus*, which came from the Greek adjective καθολικός (*katholikos*), meaning "universal". This adjective comes from a Greek phrase καθόλου (*katholou*), meaning "on the whole" or "in general", and is a combination of the Greek words κατά, which means "about" and ὅλος, which means "whole". The term "Catholic" was first used to describe the Christian Church in the early Second Century. I understand the Church, at her core, to be all-encompassing, outward-looking and inclusive. Having said that, this doesn't necessarily mean I believe all Catholics always represent the Church in this way. I understand that there are many who have had a less than positive experience of Catholic priests and people.

Marie Collins is a practising Catholic and clerical abuse survivor. In 2012 Marie was kind enough to contribute a reflection to a book of Stations of the Cross and Resurrection that I was putting together. In her writing, she reflects that the pain of what happened to her was made worse by the fact that the Catholic Church chose to protect her abuser rather than her. Marie explained, "I felt abandoned by the Church that had been the one certainty in my life. I could not bring myself to enter a church, these buildings were just hollow reminders of the past, they reminded me of what was lost, and they had no meaning for me". But she went on to write about how she has been able to come back to and remain a part of the Catholic Church, "Standing on a beach alone one day, watching the waves crash on the shore, I struggled with these thoughts. My faith in God had not changed; I was surrounded by his wonderful creation. I felt him all around me. I knew then that whatever the future would hold I would not be alone on my journey…" (Marie Collins, "Jesus appears to two disciples on the road to Emmaus", in Lucy Russell (ed.), *Journeying with Jesus: Personal Reflections on the Stations of the Cross and Resurrection*, (London: Bloomsbury, 2012), 74. The Catholic Church is not perfect, choices have been made which have caused immense pain and suffering. But like Marie, I remain a part of the Catholic Church because I have faith, and because it is my Church: it is formed by, and belongs to, the people.

Marie felt God's presence as she watched the waves crashing onto the shore. I have experienced the real presence in creation. I also find the real presence in church and at Mass. A school friend once likened going to Mass with taking an indigestion remedy: "It's like taking antacid for the mind and soul. I go in feeling stressed out, and emerge calm." The word "liturgy" originally meant a "public work" or a "service in the name of or on behalf of the people." In the Christian tradition it means the participation of the People of God in the work of God. It says in Psalm 119:164 that the people of Israel interrupted their work "seven times a day" to praise God. Jesus, who was brought up as a Jew, took part in the liturgy and prayers of his people. He taught his disciples to pray, and gathered them in the upper room to celebrate the liturgy of all liturgies: the gift of himself in the Last Supper, when he said, "Do this in memory of me". The Eucharist is a collective remembering of the Last Supper. Jesus continues his work in, with, and through his Church today through the liturgy. In the New Testament the word "liturgy" refers not only to the celebration of divine worship, but also to the proclamation of the Gospel and to active charity. Going to Mass does many things for me. It gives me time to sit quietly, reflect and pray. It's a rendezvous with Jesus that reminds me that God loves me. It inspires me to go out afterwards and keep trying. The fact that the format of the Mass remains the same, with the same prayers, can also be of great comfort at difficult times. I have always found Requiem Masses easier to bear than other funeral services I have been to, because I can "hold on" to the structure of the liturgy: the format and prayers. I know what is coming next, and so I don't feel as though I am in freefall.

Your eyes beheld my unformed substance

Psalm 139:16a

Faith is both a journey and a relationship. These days I define myself in terms of my relationships, firstly with and to God. I am also a mother, wife, daughter, sister, aunt, cousin and friend. I haven't always defined myself in this way. Especially before I had my children, when I defined myself by what I did, as many of us do. I was a teacher, a PhD student, and then a lecturer in Education. Interestingly, becoming a student again, having spent three years teaching, impacted my identity at the time. I can remember not even knowing what to wear as I moved out of a professional role and back into student life. What we wear says something about who (we think) we are. Clothing can empower and disempower. I did some anthropology as an undergraduate and remember a seminar on this which discussed why, when we go into hospital, we are asked to change into hospital gowns. There is a practical element here, but there is also an element of control. Putting on a hospital gown clearly defines us as a patient, there are often associated feelings around a loss of dignity, personal identity, and feeling exposed. Putting on a hospital gown can be disempowering. When I became a student again, a suit felt too formal, jeans didn't feel formal enough. I had to reposition myself and work out who I was and what to wear. The opportunity to complete a PhD was a privilege, but it took a while to work out where I fitted in. It felt like a loss of status, but I also didn't feel worthy of the opportunity. I thought that I should be doing something more useful, and that I would have made more of a difference if I had stayed in the classroom. It took a while to readjust. Having completed my research degree, I taught in the Educational Studies Department at Goldsmiths College, University of London. Now I felt at home here, where I had completed my PhD. I was doing something I enjoyed and felt was worthwhile. It was while I had been completing my research that my MS was diagnosed. The staff I worked alongside accepted me as I was. They never commented if I came in wearing an eye patch (because I had double vision), they let me get on with what I was doing. When I got married we moved to the south-Kent coast. So by the time I had James, I decided I would have to give up working in London. I did a bit of work as a visiting tutor, teaching a Primary PGCE course on school history and contributing to the odd Saturday School, but in the days before the fast train link, the journey was just too long. So motherhood came with not only its own transformative influence on my identity, it also signalled the end of my academic career. Until this point, I hadn't had time to sit and worry about the MS. My condition didn't define me, I was an academic and had a professional career to focus on and distract me from myself. Being Dr Lucy Russell was what defined me. Away from the Academy, I didn't use my title. After all, as Philip Hensher wrote in an article for *The Independent*, unless you're a medical doctor or an employed academic, you look a bit of an idiot if you call yourself "doctor" (13 February 2007). So I was "Mrs" now. And a mum. And there was nothing to distract me from the overwhelming responsibility of motherhood, apart from quietly worrying about the progression of the MS. Working had focused my attention on something else.

I know of those with various diagnoses who continue to work. One friend of mine who has a form of blood cancer teaches part time, despite some suggesting that she should put herself and her children first and consider stopping. I understand that she is putting herself and her children first by carrying on teaching. Illnesses and their treatment can be tiring and isolating, but leading as normal a life as possible helps. Of course we are not just what we do, but our employment undoubtedly impacts who we are. Whenever we meet someone new, this is usually the first question asked of us after we have given them our name. The desire to carry on working when living with a condition like MS is about maintaining a sense of normality and purpose. Working is an opportunity to re-build self-esteem and have a focus outside whatever condition you are living with. Our employment is often more meaningful than the pay cheque. Careers like teaching are bound up with our values, and so are important in defining who we are. Our personal identity is affected by our values.

In your book were written all the days that were formed for me, when none of them as yet existed

PSALM 139:16B

My diagnosis of MS changed me in some ways, changed my outlook, and shaped who I am. Motherhood changed my life, and revealed to me different aspects of who I am. Who I am in essence has been exposed by my priorities for my children. I am a Catholic mother with a passionate belief and interest in education. Shortly after James was born a newspaper editor asked me to write an article about how, as a mother, you can keep a spiritual life going while handling the demands of a young family. At that point, I wasn't sure a spiritual life was possible with a new baby. My priorities changed the moment I had James. I had a completely different view of the world and was utterly consumed by him. My Mass attendance was erratic as I adapted to my new vocation. Life totally revolved around my baby son. An older friend of mine had warned me that life was going to change as she congratulated me on the news of my pregnancy. I had smiled and nodded in agreement, thinking about a few nights of broken sleep and learning how to change nappies. By the time James was born I had all the baby paraphernalia; the cot, baby bath, pram and car seat. James would be sleeping in our bedroom for most of his first year, but his room was decorated, ready and waiting. I was ready and waiting too, or at least I thought I was. My friend was a mother of four and grandmother of nine, but nothing she could have said would have prepared me mentally or spiritually for the overwhelming sense of love and responsibility that arrived with James. I naively thought that life would carry on much as before except that I would have a baby to care for. But life changed: permanently and immediately. Olympic athlete Jessica Ennis Hill has talked about no longer defining herself as a sportswoman since she had her son. When a child is born, so is a mother. It's like a hand clap. The two come together in the same instant: clap! I was no longer the most important person in my life. James was. In those early days I was utterly overwhelmed by a sense of awe and wonder as I gazed at James. He affirmed my faith. Prayer might not have been possible at scheduled points in the day, but when I pushed the vacuum cleaner around, the noise of the vacuum drowned out the rest, and gave me the opportunity to say a few prayers. Like a lot of new mums, I lost myself for a while. Looking after myself fell by the wayside at first. To tell the truth, it took a long time to remember who I am and what I like. I put the children first at whatever cost to me, not realising the importance of self-nurturance and caring about myself as I cared for others, so that I could care for others. I'm not the mother I thought I would be. Is any mother? Julia Samuel has said, "The image I had of myself as a mother was a kind of jam-making, home mother who sewed on all the name tapes and did everything. And that wasn't the mother I turned out to be. I was a working mother, I was an impatient mother, I'm a loving mother" (*Desert Island Discs*, BBC Radio 4, 6 March 2015). I have made jam twice in the past ten years, and have enjoyed doing it. I try and sew on name tapes, but usually resort to a permanent marker. I'm not sure any of us are the kind of mother we imagined we would be. I think motherhood can be described as a journey of self-discovery. It came as a surprise to me in the children's earlier years when I realised that not only was it possible to have a spiritual life and a new baby, but that having a baby actually deepened my spirituality. As James grew, I started seeing all things new through his eyes. Witnessing and encouraging the awakening of James' spirituality as we went on walks to look for cats, or played on a pebbly beach in winter, left me wondering at creation. When you get beyond the routine, motherhood is very creative. It is about sharing with God in the creation of a new human being. My main priority as a mother has been ensuring that James and Edgar are aware of God's presence in their lives.

One afternoon, I was walking along the seafront with the boys. Edgar was in the pram. James, who was nearly four, was walking with me. We took a stroll down the pier. Now, I hadn't realised James couldn't actually see the sea when we were on the pier. "What are these holes for?" he asked. "They're for when it rains, the water drains away into the sea," I told him. "The sea?!" "Yes. The sea?!" "Yes. Let me lift you up to have a closer look. We are walking over the sea – the pier is like a bridge." "It's the sea! It's green!" "Yes." I smiled. We inspected all (125) drainage holes along the pier. As we walked back down the pier on that particular afternoon, I thought, just because you can't see something, doesn't mean it isn't there. And if you want to find something, it is very helpful to be shown where to look. Otherwise, there's a danger of missing it altogether.

We have made sure that the children have been introduced to a range of activities and experiences, and are actively encouraged in any that they have shown a particular interest in and aptitude for. One of Edgar's talents is certainly sport. This has had an impact on our Sunday mornings because that's when rugby takes place. Edgar can make the ten o'clock training sessions on a Sunday morning if he leaves with his Dad straight after Mass. Sometimes we take him to Mass on Saturday evening so that he can play away games on a Sunday morning. But when it came time for his First Holy Communion preparation, some away games had to be missed because he had to be at the nine o'clock Mass on a Sunday morning. "What are you doing to that kid?" remarked his coach when my husband informed him of this. I enjoy watching Edgar play sports and using his God-given talents. What we are doing is giving him a choice, he can choose to accept or reject his faith as an adult. But if we had never introduced him (or James) to any faith and spirituality, it would undoubtedly be more difficult later, for them to see the sea from the pier. What I want them to know is that rugby, and everything else, will pass away. But God will remain constant in their lives. St Teresa of Avila said: "Let nothing disturb you, Let nothing frighten you, All things are passing: God never changes." And to this end, the children won't be sitting the Kent Test and going to a Grammar School, they will attend the local Catholic secondary school. Who I am is someone who supports Catholic, comprehensive education.

Search me, O God, and know my heart; test me and know my thoughts

PSALM 139:23

Sometimes I get emails for another Dr Lucy Russell. She's a child psychologist. We have very similar email addresses. Hers is the same as mine, but for the fact she includes her middle initial (which, coincidentally, is also the same as mine). The emails which are intended for her that land in my inbox are usually from patients, so I forward them to her (without reading them!). We have never met. I used the Internet to find her email address, and in so doing I found out that we have more in common than our names. We have both had our work reviewed in the Education press. Lucy has written an online course for ten-year-olds called *Thinkerbud*, to help them deal with the stress of the eleven plus.

James was in Year 3 when he first spoke to me about these tests, "Mummy, what happens if you don't finish it before the end of the time?" I took a deep breath. What did I want for him? When James was just a few months old I can remember looking up Independent schools and Steiner schools, wanting to give him the very best education and opportunities I perhaps didn't have. I failed the Kent Test. But as James approached school age, it dawned on me that he didn't need anything different from that which I had had. "Do you know, if you go to daddy's school, you don't even have to do the test. Daddy's school is for everyone."

I could see the look of relief on his face, he smiled, "Well, I want to go to daddy's school then." Daddy is the Head of Humanities at the local Catholic secondary school; which is the same school that I went to.

In the write-up about *Thinkerbud* on the *Everlief* website, it says:

Unfortunately exams make us stressed and the expectation around this exam in particular can be quite hard on such young children.

Will they get to go to the best school? Will they get to go with their friends? Many parents buy in additional coaching for their children but to date there has been little to help children understand and cope with the stress of it all.

"11-Plus Exam Stress",
3 October 2016

My namesake is more than aware of the stress involved with the Kent Test. I worry about what we are doing to our children by putting them under such pressure. It is a pressure that extends to us as parents. We want the very best for our children. We want them to be able to achieve all we did and more. But what is education for? Being bright and well-educated doesn't necessarily make us good or happy people. Dr Haim Ginott was a psychologist and child therapist. In his book, *Teacher and Child*, he includes an epilogue, which is a letter written to educators by a Holocaust survivor:

I am a survivor of a concentration camp. My eyes saw what no person should witness: gas chambers built by learned engineers. Children poisoned by educated physicians. Infants killed by trained nurses. Women and babies shot by high school and college graduates.

So, I am suspicious of education.

My request is:

Help your children become human. Your efforts must never produce learned monsters, skilled psychopaths or educated Eichmanns.
Reading, writing, and arithmetic are important only if they serve to make our children more humane.

Haim Ginott, *Teacher and Child*
(New York: Collier Books, 1993) 317

After the beheadings of twenty-one Coptic Christians in Libya in February 2015, Bishop Angaelos, head of the Coptic Church in the UK, spoke of the need to raise awareness of the sanctity of life and the equal value of every person. I want my children to be able to function in the world and to have the ability to relate to everybody. I want them to respect others and to be respected. As it says in *The Catholic School*, "knowledge is not to be considered as a means of material prosperity and success, but as a call to serve and be responsible for others" (Congregation for Catholic Education, *The Catholic School* (Rome, 1977) 63.

And lead me in the way everlasting
Psalm 139:24b

Since becoming a mother I have felt that responsibility for others even more keenly. Everybody is somebody's child, and I know how I would want someone else to care for and treat my own children in my absence. I have understood Mary the Mother of Jesus better in this sense, as our universal mother, since I have had my own children. There are people older than me, old enough to be my parents, to whom I have responded as a mother when I have seen their vulnerability. After a Requiem Mass I had attended in my parish, I found the adult son of the elderly parishioner whom the Requiem Mass was for, in tears in a quiet corner of the presbytery garden. As I walked by on my way into the parish office I squeezed his arm, made eye contact, and told him he'd read well during the Mass. He looked me in the eye and nodded. I knew his mum a little bit. She had been a member of the Mothers' Prayer Group. This is a movement which was formed in 1995 to help mothers and grandmothers who wished to pray together for their children and grandchildren and to find the support they needed. The movement is not exclusively Catholic, it has the support and blessing of Christian leaders of all denominations. You don't even have to be a mother to join a Mothers' Prayer Group, you can join a group and pray for the world's children. With Mothers' Prayer Groups active globally, there are people praying for the world's children every minute of every day. All women, whether they have children or not, can fulfil the role of mothers and be part of a universal motherhood. Though perhaps this should be a universal parenthood, because mothering isn't exclusive to women either. When Bob Geldof became the legal guardian of his ex-wife's baby daughter, Tiger Lily Hutchence, the readers of *Prima Baby* magazine nominated him as the best celebrity mum of the year. The magazine went on to award Geldof a new title of "honorary Mum".

One thing I didn't give up when I became a mum was my writing. James and I arrived home from the maternity hospital on the same day as the set of proofs for my first book. I worked on these during the first weeks of James' life, as he slept in his Moses basket next to me. After my first book was published, I wrote a second book about the experience of completing a research degree. For a time I managed to write book reviews and an article or two about education, but now I had left the Educational Studies Department at Goldsmiths College, and couldn't really write for the education press any longer. Inspiration for my writing comes from the conversations I have and the life I am living. I still wrote about education, but from a much less academic point of view. Now I began to write for the Church press about what the children were teaching me.

Earlier in this chapter I reflected that I find God in creation as well as at Mass. There is a third place where I find the real presence, and that is in the Arts and Humanities. It is in my writing. I have numerous conversations with God while I am thinking about what I am writing. I write in complete silence, with perhaps only the sound of the birds and the wind chimes in the garden, which I hear through the open door. There is nothing lovelier than those sounds and the gentle breeze. Perhaps it is there, in the silence, that I find God. We are all blessed with gifts and talents. In the Parable of the Talents (Matthew 25:14-30) the master gives each of the servants what he thinks they are able to deal with. He does not give them any instructions about what to do with the talents, he assumes they know what is expected of them, but is disappointed in the servant who hides the money because he has not made the best of what he is given. Of course in the time of Jesus a "talent" was a large amount of money. But this parable is not only about money. God gives us gifts and talents to use freely, and he expects us to use them well. I consider writing to be my God-given talent, and hope that I am fulfilling what is expected of me. Part of my identity comes from my writing, which helps me through trickier times. I find that writing is a good distraction from the ups and downs of life, and a good way to record memories and organise my thoughts. I hope that you find what is written in these pages of interest, and perhaps of some help.

Who you are is about being true to yourself, and following your heart.

Chapter Two

I am worthy in the eyes of God

Trust in the Lord, and do good; so you will live in the land, and enjoy security.

Take delight in the Lord, and he will give you the desires of your heart.

Commit your way to the Lord; trust in him, and he will act.

He will make your vindication shine like the light, and the justice of your cause like the noonday.

Our steps are made firm by the Lord, when he delights in our way; though we stumble, we shall not fall headlong, for the Lord holds us by the hand.

Psalm 37:3-6, 23-24

The singer Jessie J was born Jessica Cornish. When she was twenty, she wrote a song called *Who You Are* with Toby Gad and Shelley Peiken. In the second verse she sings about not losing yourself in the blur of the stars, but instead following your dreams and your heart, and being true to yourself. It's an important and rather beautiful message. We are not all the same and we don't need to follow the crowd.

The inspiration for this song came at the end of a three-month trip to Los Angeles. Jessie had been shunted from studio to studio with various producers. "I'm very much someone who lives to be happy," Jessie told Elisa Bray for an article in *The Independent*, "I'm not just about the parties and I know so-and-so – I'm not that girl. So I looked in the mirror and started to cry and said, "Who am I? Music is my therapy" (Elisa Bray, "Jessie J – The girl from Essex who plans to take the pop world by storm" *The Independent*, 10 December 2010). In the same article, Jessie talked about her school days and following her dreams. Writing and performing music could be described as her vocation.

The literal meaning of the word vocation is a "call". But a vocation is more than an ordinary call. It's a call from God. Vocation is about what we are called to do in life, it is also about who we are called to be. Some might describe Jessie's experience in LA as a "stumble" (Psalm 37:24) which led to her writing this very successful track. *Who You Are* is about being true to yourself, and following your heart. The lyrics in Jessie's song are striking and she warns about losing yourself trying to conform to the expectations of others.

Do you know who you are? How well do you really know yourself? Just before I sat down to begin writing this Chapter, I had an email, asking me for a one sentence attribution for myself (in a maximum of twenty words) to go at the end of an article I had written. It took me a few minutes to think about this, and come up with something I was happy with. I went for: "Lucy Russell is a writer and author. She is mum to two sons and has a keen interest in Education". When we are asked who we are, it is most likely that we will respond with our name, job or role, and where we are from. But we are more than this. In St Paul's

Letter to the Colossians he writes, "You have died, and your life is hidden with Christ in God" (Colossians 3:3). I don't know that I know myself fully. What I do know is that my diagnosis of MS has helped me to understand better who I am. As I write this book, I am beginning to see identification as a gift from God. Through my relationships, and through my MS, there has been a process of revelation. Some of my identity, hidden in Christ, has been revealed to me.

In psychology, sociology, anthropology and philosophy, "identity" is the conception, qualities, beliefs and expressions that make a person. So, "identity" is about who a person is. To a large extent our identities are formed through relationships with significant people in our lives. I have a friend who will tell you that he knows who he is, because he knows what he is not. And what he is not, is his own father. My friend rejected his dad's politics and prejudices when he was five years old, and his father told him his friend couldn't come to play, because he was Jewish. Having formed an opinion about his dad's attitudes and judgements, my friend has spent his life defining his position, and himself, as a polar opposite to all that his father stood for.

As the sociologists, psychologists and anthropologists, will tell you, we either aspire to the characteristics of others, or wish to dissociate from them, and that this is how our identities are formed. If our identity depends on our relationships, then it can't be static, our identities must change and develop through our relationships with others. This also means that our identity is not just our identity, we are not only who we choose to be. We are also who we are for other people: I am a mother, a wife, a daughter. My identity is formed through these roles, and others. What about Jesus' identity? He was a son, a friend and a teacher.

Jesus' identity shows itself through his actions and behaviour towards those he meets. But Jesus' identity is formed not only by what he said and did, but also in the way that those around him responded to him, and in the way his life is recorded in the Gospels, and interpreted by early Church leaders like St Paul. Jesus' identity is also impacted by the way we interpret and respond to him through the Gospels. It also follows that if our identities are formed through our relationships, then our relationship with Jesus influences who we are. But if we are going to have a relationship with Jesus, first we have to get to know him.

Trust in the Lord, and do good; so you will live in the land, and enjoy security

Psalm 37:3

So, who was Jesus? Who is Jesus? Unlike the question, "does God exist?" few people question whether or not Jesus existed. Although, it is quite amazing how many people think that Father Christmas was involved in the Nativity. *The Telegraph* reported in December 2013 that one in twenty Britons think that Father Christmas makes an appearance in the Bible, a proportion which rises to ten per cent among the twenty-five to thirty-five age group. A significant number of people apparently also think that Mary and Joseph might have brightened up the stable with a Christmas tree. More than two thousand people of all ages were polled on their knowledge of the Christmas story in the *ComRes* survey conducted on behalf of the Christian Institute (John Bingham, "Father Christmas granted a walk-on part in the Bible", *The Telegraph*, 21 December 2013). So, when my twenty-two-year-old Cambridge Graduate cousin told me she didn't believe that Jesus is the Son of God, and I responded, "Of course that's up to you, but you can't deny he was an incredible teacher and a radical", I shouldn't have been surprised that she was amazed that Jesus actually existed as an historical figure. Given the evidence of the *ComRes* survey, there may well be a number of people who think of Jesus as a mythical character like Father Christmas in whom you either believe, or you don't.

But there is no question that Jesus of Nazareth existed as a person. Jesus was born near Palestine towards the end of the reign of Herod the Great. We don't know the actual date of Jesus' birth, but it was almost certainly not 25 December, and Father Christmas was certainly not there. Jesus' parents were called Mary and Joseph, and his family tree went back to King David, who lived about 1000-961 BC. Jesus was brought up in a town called Nazareth in southern Galilee, about one hundred miles north of Jerusalem and a few miles from Sepphoris, which was the largest city in Galilee. Since 63 BC Palestine had been under Roman occupation, as part of the Roman Empire. We don't actually know very much about Jesus' early years. He was brought up in the Jewish faith, and he probably learned to read and write in a local synagogue. There is one story in the Gospel of St Luke which tells us something about Jesus while he was growing up. When he was about twelve he went with his family and others from Nazareth to celebrate the Passover in Jerusalem. At the end of the festival everyone set off for home. Maybe Mary assumed Jesus was with Joseph and the men, and Joseph assumed he was with Mary and the women. But after a day of travelling, Mary and Joseph looked for Jesus among their relations and friends, and realised he wasn't with the caravan at all. Mary and Joseph returned to Jerusalem and searched frantically for him. After three days, they discovered him in the Temple, where he was listening to the teachers and asking them questions: "And all who heard him were amazed at his understanding and his answers" (Luke 2:47). St Luke tells us that when Mary and Joseph found Jesus in the Temple they were overcome, as any parent would be. Mary reacts like any mother, "Child, why have you treated us like this? Look, your father and I have been searching for you in great anxiety" (Luke 2:48). Jesus himself is unfazed, basically saying, "Well, where did you think I would be?" This account reveals something about the kind of person Jesus was: he is intelligent and has confidence. But he is also sensitive to those around him, because having been told off by his mother for worrying herself and Joseph, St Luke tells us that he returned with them to Nazareth and "was obedient to them" (Luke 2:51).

C S Lewis would take issue with me suggesting to my cousin that it was her choice whether or not to believe that Jesus was the Son of God, but that it is undeniable that Jesus was a great teacher and radical. Lewis writes in his book, *Mere Christianity*:

I am trying here to prevent anyone from saying the really foolish thing that people often say about him [Jesus]: "I am ready to accept Jesus as a great moral teacher, but I don't accept his claim to be God". That is the one thing we must not say. A man who was merely a man and said the sort of things Jesus said would not be a great moral teacher. He would either be a lunatic – on a level with a man who says he is a poached egg – or else he would be the Devil of hell. You must make your choice. Either this man was, and is, the Son of God, or else a madman or something worse. You can shut him up for fool, you can spit at him and kill him as a demon; or you can fall at his feet and call him Lord and God. But let us not come up with any patronising nonsense about his being a great human teacher. He has not left that option open to us. He did not intend to.

C S Lewis, *Mere Christianity*
(London: William Collins, 2016) 52

Take delight in the Lord, and he will give you the desires of your heart

PSALM 37:4

So, who does Jesus say he is? A good starting place for an answer to this question is St John's Gospel. In John 8:58, Jesus says, "Very truly, I tell you, before Abraham was, I am". And in John 10:30, Jesus says, "The Father and I are one". Which prompts the question, "Who is the Father?" The Father is God, and God just is. God is creative. The book of Genesis opens by telling us both of these things: that God is, and that God is creative: "In the beginning when God created the heavens and the earth..." (Genesis 1:1). "God is love" (1 John 4:16b). God is wisdom (1 Corinthians 2:6-16). God's creative energy continues; creation is ongoing. God is the potter, we are the clay (Isaiah 64:8). This means that we are moulded and fashioned throughout our lives, just like a piece of clay on a potter's wheel. God knows what the finished work should be, but we are not there yet. I thought I was shaping up to be a vase before my diagnosis of MS, but God is still working at the potter's wheel. God has a clear idea of what I am being created to be. I don't know for certain what God's plan is, perhaps I'm going to be a jug. When James was born, I used to rock him and sing him to sleep, and one of the songs I sang him (as well as *Nellie the Elephant*) was *Abba Father* by Carey Landry. In this wonderfully meditative hymn we invite the Father to mould and fashion us, into the image of Jesus, the Potter's Son.

We are left in little doubt by St John, that Jesus is the Son of God. At the beginning of his Gospel, John writes, "In the beginning was the Word, and the Word was with God, and the Word was God" (John 1:1). In John 1:14, it says, "And the Word became flesh and lived among us, and we have seen his glory, the glory as of a father's

45

only son, full of grace and truth". Towards the end of John's Gospel, Thomas the Twin says to the resurrected Jesus, "My Lord and my God!" (John 20:28). John is not alone in his belief in the identity of Jesus. In St Paul's letter to Titus, Paul describes Jesus as, "...our great God and Saviour, Jesus Christ" (Titus 2:13). And then there is Peter's view about Jesus' identity, which is revealed when Jesus asks his disciples who the people think he is:

Now when Jesus came into the district of Caesarea Philippi, he asked his disciples, "Who do the people say the Son of Man is?" And they said, "Some say John the Baptist, but others Elijah, and still others Jeremiah or one of the prophets." He said to them, "But who do you say that I am?" Simon Peter answered, "You are the Messiah, the Son of the living God." And Jesus answered him, "Blessed are you, Simon son of Jonah! For flesh and blood has not revealed this to you, but my Father in heaven. And I tell you, you are Peter, and on this rock I will build my Church, and the gates of Hades will not prevail against it."

MATTHEW 16:13-19

One of the interesting things about this piece of scripture is all the possible answers that the disciples give Jesus. But Jesus isn't having an identity crisis. He knows who he is, confident in his description of himself as the "Son of Man". What Jesus wants to know is whether the people have recognised his identity. And in fairness to the people, they have recognised something special about Jesus. They might not identify him as the Messiah, but they are making comparisons between him and the prophets. Alright, says Jesus, that's what the people think, now tell me who you think I am. Here the disciples have an advantage over the people, because their relationship with Jesus is closer. While the people might not be sure, Peter recognises who Christ is. It is through Peter's relationship with Jesus, and Jesus' relationship with Peter, that each is able to identify the other: "You are the Messiah" says Peter, and, "you are Peter" says Jesus. Remember, until this point, Peter is actually Simon, son of Jonah. His identity is changed and shaped by Christ, now Simon Peter becomes Peter, the rock upon whom Jesus will build his Church.

The former Archbishop of Canterbury, Dr Rowan Williams, has said that Christian identity is about belonging in a place that Jesus defines for us, "By living in that place, we come in some degree to share his identity, to bear his name and to be in the same relationships he has with God and the world" (Rowan Williams, "What We Mean By Christian Identity – *World Council of Churches Address*", 17 February 2006). So, how do we move to a place defined for us by Jesus? In Christ? How do we move to a place defined for us by Jesus? In the United States in the 1990s, the phrase "What would Jesus do?" became popular with Evangelical Christians who used the phrase as a reminder to act in a way that demonstrates the love of Jesus. Thinking about what Jesus might do, is a good guiding principle when trying to root our lives and identities in him:

By standing in the place of Christ, it is possible to live in such intimacy with God that no fear or failure can ever break God's commitment to us, and to live in such a degree of mutual gift and understanding that no human conflict or division need bring us to uncontrollable violence and mutual damage. From here, you can see what you need to see to be at peace with God and with God's creation; and also what you need to be at peace with yourself, acknowledging your need of mercy and re-creation.

Rowan Williams, "What We Mean By Christian Identity – *World Council of Churches Address*" (17 February 2006)

Our steps are made firm by the Lord, when he delights on our way

PSALM 37:23

Many of us are searching. I was still searching, floundering, when I began writing this book. I believe there is within us a space, which only God can fill. There is a terrific quote in *This Is Water: Some Thoughts, Delivered on a Significant Occasion, about Living a Compassionate Life* by David Foster Wallace:

There is no such thing as not worshipping. Everybody worships. The only choice we get is what to worship. And the compelling reason for maybe choosing some sort of god or spiritual-type thing to worship – be it JC or Allah, be it YHWH or the Wiccan Mother Goddess, or the Four Noble Truths, or some inviolable set of ethical principles – is that pretty much anything else you worship will eat you alive. If you worship money and things, if they are where you tap real meaning in life, then you will never have enough, never feel you have enough. It's the truth. Worship your body and beauty and sexual allure and you will always feel ugly. And when time and age start showing, you will die a million deaths before they finally grieve you. On one level, we all know this stuff already. It's been codified as myths, proverbs, clichés, epigrams, parables; the skeleton of every great story. The whole trick is keeping the truth up front in daily consciousness.

DAVID FOSTER WALLACE, *THIS IS WATER: SOME THOUGHTS, DELIVERED ON A SIGNIFICANT OCCASION, ABOUT LIVING A COMPASSIONATE LIFE* (NEW YORK: LITTLE BROWN AND COMPANY, 2009)

I used to find fulfilment in my work, but after I had James, I admit that I had an identity crisis. I found myself juggling ironing, housework and caring for James, while all the time comparing myself to other mothers and wishing I was a better, more together, version of myself. The truth, I have learned, is that we can't find fulfilment in ourselves, any more than we can find it in the worship of money or our own body. And, why not? Well, because we were created for and by God, and like any piece of art, we reflect the talents, or the glory, of the artist who created us. There is more about art, creativity and God in Chapter Five. As I write this, there is a verse from Graham Kendrick's hymn, *Shine Jesus Shine* playing in my head:

As we gaze on your kingly brightness

So our faces display your likeness

Ever changing from glory to glory

Mirrored here may our lives tell your story

Shine on me....

It is in the artist's reflected glory that we hope to become glorified. According to St Paul in his letter to the Philippians (3:20-21), our citizenship is in heaven, and when Jesus returns, he will transform our bodies to be like "the body of his glory". The Christian viewpoint, that we'll come on to in Chapter Three, is a much longer view. The First Letter of St John warns us about trying to define ourselves in the world, rather than in the one who created the world:

Do not love the world or the things in the world. The love of the Father is not in those who love the world; for all that is in the world – the desire of the flesh, the desire of the eyes, the pride in riches – comes not from the Father but from the world. And the world and its desire are passing away, but those who do the will of God live forever.

1 JOHN 2:15-17

Unless we seek to find our identity in Christ, we are looking to find ourselves in something else. Which, as Wallace has pointed out, is a fairly thankless and fruitless task. If we root our identity in Christ, we don't need to be anxious or fear the future any more. All we have to do is put Jesus first, and just be in the presence of Christ. This is summed up in the Gospel story of Martha and Mary. While Martha is busy serving her guests, Mary, sitting at the feet of Jesus and listening to him, has, in that instance, "chosen the better part":

Now as they went on their way, he entered a certain village, where a woman named Martha welcomed him into her home. She had a sister named Mary, who sat at the Lord's feet and listened to what he was saying. But Martha was too distracted by her many tasks; so she came to him and asked, "Lord, do you not care that my sister has left me to do all the work by myself? Tell her then to help me." But the Lord answered her, "Martha, Martha, you are worried and distracted by many things; there is need of only one thing. Mary has chosen the better part, which will not be taken away from her."

LUKE 10:38-42

Martha is distracted from the presence of Christ because she is too busy *doing* things for him to be still and listen to him. There is a bit of Martha and Mary in all of us, they are the two sides of ourself. We need to be able to choose when to be more like Mary and less like Martha, when to be doing things for Christ and when to be still and listen to him. We are often so busy doing things for God that we forget to stop and listen to what God is saying to us. I am trying to be still more often each day to listen to the God who is present at the centre of my being.

So, when I am asked who I am, my response needs to include my religious identity. I am Catholic by religion. Christian by faith. English by nationality. British by citizenship. European by culture. In my heart, my Catholicism and Christianity very definitely come first. St Paul writes in his letter to the Galatians that our faith will grow stronger as we focus our identity in

Christ. We all have a personal vocation, but discerning this, and our own identity, isn't easy. We can feel a bit like the apostles waiting for the Holy Spirit in the upper room. How many of us have woken up dreading the day ahead? Very few of us feel we have a calling, and so we often don't think about our lives in terms of vocation. But what if the school run, the daily grind, and the colleagues we find difficult, are all actually viewed as something God has willed as part of his plan? Rather than trying to define myself by the opinions and values of others (something Jessie J warns about in her song, *Who We Are*), or by my own feelings and desires, I am trying to let God define me, and tell me who I am. If we want to discern our vocation, the first thing we need to do is stop trying to be something we are not intended to be, and instead of thinking, "What would I prefer", think about the question, "What does God want me to be?". My MS has taught me that I am not in control (there is more about that in Chapter Three!), and that God knows me better than I know myself.

When he took part in Radio 4's *Desert Island Discs*, comedian and actor, Jack Dee, told Kirsty Young that at the age of twenty-one or twenty-two he was seriously considering becoming a priest:

> I was becoming increasingly turned in on myself and depressed and had turned to religion as a place to hide away from what I was feeling. I felt massively conflicted in what I was doing in my life. I knew I was going hopelessly wrong.

Desert Island Discs, BBC Radio 4 (11 May 2014)

At this point in his life Jack experienced a frustration at not knowing what he was aiming for, where was his life going? He felt as though he was going in the wrong direction. He spent hours sitting in a church. Interestingly, Kirsty Young asked him when the moment of clarity came: it was when working in a restaurant in Covent Garden, surrounded by drama students, actors and performers. Someone asked him one day what he did performance-wise. "The fact they had assumed I was one of them made me realise I always had been one of them." Jack himself describes the moment he realised he was a comedian as an epiphany. His account of how he found his way into comedy sounds similar to a religious experience, "I had a very strong sense of identity that was always kind of speaking to me" he said. But he didn't hear this until his vocation was revealed to him through his relationship with other actors and performers. While not a religious man, Jack describes himself as a man of faith. It is through our relationships with each other and with God that we begin to see who we really are. It was in recognising Jesus, that Peter discovered who he was. If we root our identity in Christ, and recognise who he is, perhaps we can also discover who we truly are.

Mary Magdalene, the disciples on the road to Emmaus, and Thomas the Twin, all take time to recognise Jesus after the Resurrection. What is interesting about the Resurrection accounts is the number of appearances Jesus makes to his friends. There are fifty days between Easter and Pentecost, during which time the disciples come to recognise their friend and believe in the Resurrection. They watch Jesus ascend to heaven, having just got used to having him around again. And then the Holy Spirit comes and changes everything. The apostles, consumed by confusion and lacking in confidence now that Jesus has gone again, had hidden themselves away. But, after receiving the Spirit they are transformed: clear and confident not only of their vocation, but also in their ability to live this out. The process of identifying Jesus as Christ, risen from the dead and ascended into heaven, has led them to this point.

Though we stumble, we shall not fall headlong, for the Lord holds us by the hand

PSALM 37:24

St Paul's own calling was unmistakable. He literally heard the voice of God:

Meanwhile Saul, still breathing threats and murder against the disciples of the Lord, went to the high priest and asked him for letters to the synagogues at Damascus…Now as he was going along and approaching Damascus, suddenly a light from heaven flashed around him. He fell to the ground and heard a voice saying to him, "Saul, Saul, why do you persecute me?" He asked, "Who are you, Lord?" The reply came, "I am Jesus, whom you are persecuting. But get up and enter the city, and you will be told what you are to do."

ACTS 9.1-6

Saul's own identity is only revealed to him when he enters a relationship with Jesus. Saul, who was also known as Paul, is known only as Paul from Acts 13:9. Saul is left behind. St Paul is a really interesting example when it comes to talking about what makes us who we are, and how our identity is hidden in Christ. In Paul's letter to the Galatians, he makes it clear that he understands that God's purpose for him was decided before he was born:

But when God, who had set me apart before I was born and called me through his grace, was pleased to reveal his Son to me, so that I might proclaim him among the Gentiles, I did not confer with any human being.

GALATIANS 1:15-16

Paul had always felt a strong call to holiness (we are all called to holiness), which is what prompted him to become a Pharisee, and to follow Mosaic Law in such a very determined way.

Paul describes himself in the Acts of the Apostles as "being zealous for God" (Acts 22:3). It was Paul's conviction about this calling that led him to persecute Christians whom he saw as a dangerous threat to the Jewish faith. The fact that God allowed early Christians to suffer as a result of Saul's convictions, raises questions about suffering and where God is during our suffering. Why did God allow Saul to persecute Christians? These are questions we will come to in the next chapter. What I want to note here is that it was the man who persecuted the first Christians, whom God had chosen to lead his Early Church. Paul's conversion is an example of God's mercy and love, Saul is forgiven for what he has done. There is another question here, if Paul's conversion had not been so dramatic, would he have become such a committed Christian? He understood God's grace and mercy, because of his experience of it. He wrote to Timothy:

I am grateful to Christ Jesus our Lord, who has strengthened me, because he judged me faithful and appointed me to his service, even though I was formerly a blasphemer, a persecutor, and a man of violence. But I received mercy because I had acted ignorantly in unbelief, and the grace of our Lord overflowed for me with the faith and love that are in Christ Jesus. The saying is sure and worthy of full acceptance, that Christ Jesus came into the world to save sinners – of whom I am the foremost. But for that very reason I received mercy, so that in me, as the foremost, Jesus Christ might display the utmost patience, making me an example to those who would come to believe in him for eternal life.　　1 Timothy 1:12-16

St Paul is an example of someone who had a calling, but didn't understand the exact nature of his calling, until he was on the road to Damascus. He knew he was being called by God, and thought this was as a Jewish Pharisee. In fact, God wanted Paul to lead the Early Church. Our moment of "epiphany", when we understand who we are and what we are being called to be, may not be as dramatic as that experienced by the apostles at Pentecost, or St Paul on the road to Damascus. So, how can we be sure we are going in the right direction? What if we, like Saul, have only got it half right? Well, we have the examples of St Peter and St Paul, who recognised Jesus and entered into a relationship with him, and then discovered who they were.

I will never forget going to see Edgar in his Year 2 class assembly about chocolate. He was in role as Willy Wonka for the assembly, as the children explained all that they had learned about the history of chocolate and Fairtrade, and acted out part of Roald Dahl's *Charlie and the Chocolate Factory*. Edgar was brilliant as Willy Wonka, but that is not why I shall remember the afternoon. I will remember it because of the reaction of one of the mothers on the playground the next day, her daughter had played an Oompa Loompa. She had been horrified to find a dead shrew in the pocket of her daughter's costume, after the little Oompa Loompa had got home. The Oompa Loompa had evidently found the dead shrew under the horse chestnut tree on the way into school on the morning of the assembly, and picked it up. I laughed, and later asked the Oompa Loompa why she had put the shrew in her pocket. She thought she could make it better. Perhaps she will grow up to be a vet. Thomas Aquinas said that the things that we love tell us what we are". God loves us, and love tells us who we are. I'm beginning not to mind the lack of control. I'm quite happy for God to be in charge, since God wants our happiness more than we do. But not being in control doesn't mean we are passive. If we care being called, it is our choice to decide whether or not to answer. Vocation is about conversation and relationship. It can be described as an ongoing conversion experience, which keeps opening our eyes to a new awareness and understanding of God's loving presence. Who we are, are God's children (1 John 3:1). I hope I can give God some of the joy that my own children and the Oompa Loompa in Edgar's class, give me, as I try to understand and become the person I am meant to be.

Sometimes the
feeling of emptiness
within us can be so
great that only God
can fill that space

Chapter Three

God knows who I am

My God, my God, why have you forsaken me?
Why are you so far from helping me, from the words of my groaning?
O my God, I cry by day, but you do not answer;
and by night, but find no rest.

Yet it was you who took me from the womb; you kept me safe on
my mother's breast.

On you I was cast from my birth, and since my mother bore me
you have been my God.

Do not be far from me, for trouble is near and there is no one to help.

Psalm 22:1-2, 9-11

Delta Goodrem wrote the song *Mistaken Identity* with Billy Mann after her experience of being diagnosed with, and having aggressive treatment for, Hodgkin's lymphoma.

In an interview for *The Guardian* in 2007, Delta told Alastair Campbell that what was interesting was that she wasn't thinking, why me? "Once I was through the initial shock, I thought, this is my next challenge and how you deal with things will determine the kind of person you are" (Alastair Campbell, "I'm fit and strong now. I feel blessed", *The Guardian*, 29 April 2007). I can identify with Delta. When I was diagnosed with MS, I was determined I should be in control of it, rather than it of me.

I tried not to be negative, and to carry on as normal. I was keen to try to make things okay for the people around me. This is the person I am. I didn't think "why me?", what I thought was, "why not me?".

My God, my God, why have you forsaken me?

PSALM 22:1A

The first line of Psalm 22 reveals a fundamental paradox: the presence of God at times when God seems most absent. Sometimes the feeling of emptiness within us can be so great that only God can fill that space. St John of the Cross talked about the idea of the dark night of the soul, and the notion that the darker it is, and the more alone you feel, the closer you may be to God. The idea puts me in mind of England in January. Earth is closest to the sun every year in early January, when it is winter in the Northern Hemisphere. It's hard to believe we are closest to the sun in the dead of winter. But we are. And we are closest to God in our own personal winters. When asked where God was during the Holocaust, Rabbi Hugo Gryn said: "God was there [in Auschwitz] himself, violated and blasphemed." I'll come back to Hugo's words again in this chapter.

There is a strand of Christian thinking that says suffering should be accepted passively and is good for the soul. This is something that Robin Baird-Smith questioned in his reflection on the twelfth Station of the Cross, *Jesus is Crucified*, in the collection I put together in 2012. Reflecting on Jesus' words from the cross, "My God, my God, why have you forsaken me?", Robin writes: "There is here more than meets the eye. Despair maybe, but also the expression of anger. The repression of anger, as the psychologists tell us emphatically, results in depression, despair"

(Robin Baird-Smith, "Jesus is Crucified", in Lucy Russell (ed.), *Journeying with Jesus: Personal Reflections on the Stations of the Cross and Resurrection* (London: Bloomsbury, 2012), 48. We are allowed to be angry (look at Job, we'll come on to him shortly). We are not expected to understand or passively accept what life throws at us. Our relationship with God enjoys the same range of emotions that are involved in any of our relationships. This chapter is about that relationship, and the presence of God in our lives during times of challenge and suffering.

A theological answer to a question about suffering and God's presence or absence during difficult times in our lives, or during genocides, war and terrorist atrocities, can seem more than a little lacking. But I have never been angry about my MS, or felt that it isn't fair. Life is life, and what God offers us is a relationship, not a rescue, at least not an earthly one. When Hagar runs away from Abram's settlement because of her harsh treatment, God finds her by a spring of water in the wilderness. God talks to her; listens to her; tells her she will be blessed with many descendants; and tells her to call her son Ishmael. Ishmael means "God hears". Hagar is abused and powerless. God tells Hagar she has been heard, but also that she should go back to Sarai and Abram. The meeting between Hagar and God is momentous. Hagar says, "Have I really seen God?" It is she who is the first person in the Bible to name God. Hagar isn't rescued from her circumstances, but God recognises her pain and her significance (Genesis 16:7-16).

Not even God's only Son is rescued from his passion and death. Jesus endured the pain and suffering of crucifixion. In St Luke's account of the crucifixion, we read that two criminals were crucified with Jesus. One, says Luke:

Kept deriding him and saying, "Are you not the Messiah? Save yourself and us!" But the other rebuked him, saying, "Do you not fear God, since you are under the same sentence of condemnation? And we indeed have been condemned justly, for we are getting what we deserve for our deeds, but this man has done nothing wrong." Then he said, "Jesus, remember me when you come into your kingdom." He replied, "Truly I tell you, today you will be with me in Paradise."

LUKE 23:39-43

It is interesting to contrast how these two criminals who are hanged with Christ, respond to him. The penitent thief is not named in the Gospels, but has become known in Christian tradition as St Dismas. Thomas Merton, in his book, *No Man is an Island*, writes about him, "The dying thief had, perhaps, disobeyed the will of God in many things: but in the most important event of his life he listened and obeyed." St Dismas had a viewpoint which looked beyond the here-and-now, asking Jesus to remember him when he comes into his kingdom. Dismas accepts the situation he is in, but is looking and hoping for a better future. The first thief puts me in mind of the modern atheist, thinking only of the here-and-now.

In 2015 Stephen Fry was interviewed by Gay Byrne on his programme *The Meaning of Life*. "Suppose it's all true, and you walk up to the pearly gates, and are confronted by God," Byrne asked, "What will Stephen Fry say to him, her, or it?" Fry replied:

I'd say, bone cancer in children? What's that about? How dare you? How dare you create a world in which there is such misery that is not our fault. It's not right, it's utterly, utterly evil. Why should I respect a capricious, mean-minded, stupid God who creates a world that is so full of injustice and pain. That's what I would say.

Fry is not alone, in 2010 David Attenborough wrote that he could not see any role for a God in the creation of life. In his words, "When the Lord is 'given credit' for having created wondrous beauty, people always mean 'beautiful things like flamingos and hummingbirds'". But, says Attenborough, "I always reply by saying that I think of a little child in East Africa with a worm burrowing through his eyeball. The worm cannot live in any other way except by burrowing through human eyeballs. And I find that totally impossible to reconcile with the notion of a divine and benevolent Creator". These are points of view which are enormously difficult. I find these statements hard to read, because they are so lacking in hope, and see life as being defined only in terms of the here-and-now. I have never viewed life like that. In his book, *Miraculous Healing: Exploring Miraculous Healing in God's Redemptive Mission* (Canada: FriesenPress, 2015), Max Sturge writes about a conversation that Gavin Reid, former Anglican Bishop of Maidstone, had with a young man in his congregation. As a little boy, Gavin's parishioner had fallen and broken his back, and as a result he spent most of his life in and out of hospital. "God is fair," this young man said to Gavin, who responded by asking how old he was. "Seventeen," came the reply. "How many years have you spent in hospital?" asked Gavin, the boy replied, "Thirteen years." "Do you think that is fair?" Gavin asked. "God has got all eternity to make it up to me," the boy replied. Like Gavin's parishioner, I feel a great sense of hope for the future, which I believe continues beyond death. However, Stephen Fry, David Attenborough, and others, would probably think we were deluding ourselves. Though I find it difficult to engage with a viewpoint which is so lacking in hope, this point of view does raise important questions: Why is there suffering? How can a loving God allow it?

Why are you so far from helping me, from the words of my groaning?

PSALM 22:1B

Theodicy is the branch of theology which answers the question of why God permits evil. In the Parable of the Weeds among the Wheat, we have one explanation:

He put before them another parable: "The kingdom of heaven may be compared to someone who sowed good seed in his field; but while everybody was asleep, an enemy came and sowed weeds among the wheat, and then went away. So, when the plants came up and bore grain, then the weeds appeared as well. And the slaves of the householder came and said to him, 'Master, did you not sow good seed in your field? Where, then, did these weeds come from?' He answered, 'An enemy has done this.' The slaves said to him, 'Then do you want us to go and gather them?' But he replied, 'No; for in gathering the weeds you would uproot the wheat along with them. Let both of them grow together until the harvest; and at harvest time I will tell the reapers, "Collect the weeds first and bind them in bundles to be burned, but gather the wheat into my barn."'

Then he left the crowds and went into the house. And his disciples approached him, saying, "Explain to us the parable of the weeds of the field." He answered, "The one who sows the good seed is the Son of Man, the field is the world, and the good seed are the children of the kingdom; the weeds are the children of the evil one, and the enemy who sowed them is the devil; the harvest is the end of the age, and the reapers are angels. Just as the weeds are collected and burned up with fire, so it will be at the end of the age. The Son of Man will send his angels, and they will collect out of his kingdom, all causes of sin and evildoers, and they will throw them into the furnace of fire, where there will be weeping and gnashing of teeth. Then the righteous will shine like the sun in the kingdom of their Father. Let anyone with ears listen!"

MATTHEW 13:24-30, 36-44

Evil and suffering are weeds which can really get a stranglehold and overshadow our lives. But those weeds don't exist by God's design or will. They were not planted by the Son of Man. So, why doesn't the one who sows the good seed let the field be weeded? Because weeding would cause the wheat to be uprooted too. God might not intervene to rid the world of evil and suffering, but God will not be the cause of any evil and suffering. There is another noteworthy point about this parable. The one who comes in the night, and plants the weeds, immediately scarpers. But the one who sowed the good seed *remains*. The field might have weeds growing amongst the good seed that he sowed, but the good farmer isn't about to go off or give up on the crop. He keeps his eye on this field. He is present as the weeds take hold and grow up among the good seeds that he has planted. I have already noted Hugo Gryn's understanding of where God was during the Holocaust. He felt God's presence in Auschwitz: "When people dethrone God and put themselves before God, God cries. He was with us at Auschwitz when I prayed as hard as I knew how" (Michael Freedland, *Everyone's Chief Rabbi*, The JC.com, [The Jewish Chronicle online], (26 May 2016). I believe we each have our own Guardian Angel. I asked a friend once what our Guardian Angels are doing while dreadful things may be happening to us. "Weeping," was his response.

In you our ancestors trusted, they trusted and you delivered them

PSALM 22:4

Jesus was honest about the presence of suffering in our lives. As is noted in John 16:33, Jesus said, "In the world you face persecution". Life is full of ups and downs. I'm not suggesting I don't struggle with some of the difficulties in my own life, or that I don't often find events reported in the news upsetting and unsettling. I don't have God's perspective and can't fully answer the question of why God allows suffering. But then, as St Paul writes in his letter to the Corinthians "For now we see in a mirror, dimly…Now I know only in part…" (1 Corinthians 13:12). God is love, the author of a good creation, not of pain and suffering.

I don't think that suffering is good in itself, but perhaps it can sometimes result in good. I can believe in God and a good creation, despite the presence of evil. My children have asked me why Good Friday is known as "*Good* Friday". How can the crucifixion of Jesus be in any way a good thing? I have told them that without Good Friday, we wouldn't have Easter Sunday. We don't need to go out of our way to emulate Christ and crucify ourselves, he has already done this for us. Besides which, no-one's life is perfect. Everyone faces challenges of one sort or another. Suffering will, inevitably, find us. But St Paul believes that when it comes our way, we can use it to our benefit. St Paul's writing is a good place to start when considering the meaning of suffering, this is something he spent some time reflecting upon.

In his letter to the Philippians, St Paul explains that his own suffering is a way of taking part in salvation. When he suffers, not only does this serve as a way to be like Christ, it is also for Christ's sake. St Paul writes, "I want to know Christ and the power of his resurrection and the sharing of his sufferings by becoming like him in his death, if somehow I may attain the resurrection from the dead" (Philippians 3:10-11). So, through his own suffering, St Paul sees himself as participating in the suffering of Christ. There is a notion here that we are being saved through the death and resurrection of Christ, so to obtain salvation and share in the resurrection, we have also to share in Christ's passion. For St Paul, suffering is an imitation of

Christ, which makes him more Christ-like. There is also another dimension to St Paul's thinking about the meaning of suffering, which I find particularly interesting; this is the idea of suffering as a way of sanctification. This means that suffering is a reminder that we are not in control, we have to trust in God.

There is an old joke that if you want to make God laugh, you should outline your plans. Delta Goodrem has written another song (with Wayne Wilkins, Stephen Kipner and Andrew Frampton) which is called, *God Laughs*. This song is about life's illusion that we are secure and everything is always going to be the same, and how it feels when that illusion is shattered by an event like a divorce. Delta sings that we are all walking on quicksand. And we are.

Much of what we consider normal and take for granted, is actually a God-given gift. "Plane! Plane!" Edgar shouted to me excitedly while pointing wildly into the sky. He was eighteen months old. I looked up, smiling. Sure enough, it was the first plane we had seen for six days, and it was flying high in the sky over our house, painting a white vapour trail across a beautiful azure canvas. It was early in the summer of 2010 and the eruption of the Icelandic volcano, *Eyjafjallajökull*, had resulted in an ash cloud which caused all kinds of travel chaos and the dumping of tonnes of vegetables and flowers bound for export from Kenya to the UK. As far as the insurance companies were concerned, the eruption of the volcano was an "act of God". It's funny how we accept these overwhelming natural events as "acts of God". As though we can believe God would be in such destruction. Although these kinds of events would appear to be uninfluenced by human hand (except in the case of extreme weather caused by global warming), they can hardly be the work of God either.

Elijah's meeting with God at Horeb is described in the First book of Kings. When Elijah reached Horeb, the mountain of God, he went into a cave and spent the night there. Then he was told:

"Go out and stand on the mountain before the Lord, for the Lord is about to pass by." Now there was a great wind, so strong that it was splitting mountains and breaking rocks in pieces before the Lord, but the Lord was not in the wind; and after the wind an earthquake, but the Lord was not in the earthquake; and after the earthquake a fire, but the Lord was not in the fire; and after the fire a sound of sheer silence. When Elijah heard it, he wrapped his face in his mantle and went out and stood at the entrance of the cave. Then there came a voice to him that said, "What are you doing here, Elijah?"

1 KINGS 19:11-13

God is in the silence and the gentle breeze. I could see God's handiwork in the impressive pictures of the Icelandic volcano. Perhaps even more wonderful is God's handiwork in humanity. Like the ability to fly around the world, we take our creation for granted. We take it for granted that we can pop to the supermarket for food grown all over the world. But while the airports were closed, journalists reported from deserted runways, obviously taken with the idea that in normal circumstances they wouldn't be allowed to report from the tarmac. Just for a moment, we remembered what an amazing achievement and opportunity aviation is. The eruption of the volcano caused a good deal of inconvenience and anxiety, and was a reminder that we are not really in control. Like such inconvenience and anxiety, pain and suffering is a reminder of our fragility, and our need to confess our dependence on God.

Yet it was you who took me from the womb; you kept me safe on my mother's breast

PSALM 22:9

I come back to some of those last words of Christ on the cross: "My God, My God, why have you forsaken me?" Jesus is nailed to the cross, asking where God is. God is nailed to the cross, utterly present in Jesus' suffering. After these words, Jesus surrenders: "Father, into your hands I commend my spirit" (Luke 23:46). Job's story is similar. The Book of Job focuses on his sufferings, and takes us to the very threshold of Job's despair. Job prays to God in his suffering, asking why God isn't doing anything to help him, demanding a response from God. And in the end, finally surrenders everything to God:

I know that you can do all things, and that no purpose of yours can be thwarted. "Who is this that hides counsel without knowledge?" Therefore I have uttered what I did not understand, things too wonderful for me, which I did not know. "Hear, and I will speak; I will question you, and you declare to me." I had heard of you by the hearing of the ear, but now my eye sees you; therefore I despise myself, and repent in dust and ashes.

JOB 42:1-6

The rawness of Job's suffering forces us to face the frailty of our own mortality. The main difference between us and Job is the illusion that we are somehow in control of our lives. We are not. Childbirth is one great proof of this. I can clearly recall sitting down and writing a "birth plan" with my midwife: what pain relief did I want? Did I want a water birth? Did my husband want to cut the cord? All of these preferences and ideals went out of the window when James got stuck and I had a couple of ambulance rides and ended up in an operating theatre. Two and a half years later, when Edgar came along, I opted for a home birth. That didn't work out either! But the point is, I was fine, and so were the boys. We were lucky enough to have the help that we needed.

Giving birth brings home St Paul's point about sanctification. You don't get to choose the moment, you are certainly not in control of events. Once I had my new baby in my arms, I wanted my control over his little life to be absolute. I wanted to watch over and protect James and Edgar always, but there are so many things which are beyond our control. What about outside influences, and the times when I couldn't be there? There comes a point when we have to hand over our parental responsibility to God, and place our trust there. Stephen Fry asked why God allows people to suffer, but no-one suffers alone. As in the Parable of the Weeds among the Wheat, God is watching over us, present during times of challenge or suffering. We might not be in control, but we are not on our own. St Luke writes:

Are not five sparrows sold for two pennies? Yet not one of them is forgotten in God's sight. But even the hairs of your head are all counted. Do not be afraid; you are of more value than many sparrows.

LUKE 12:6-8

So, suffering can be seen as a way of increasing our trust in God, as St Paul writes to the Corinthians, we suffer "so that we would rely not on ourselves but on God who raises the dead" (2 Corinthians 1:9). St Paul goes on here to mention the importance of prayer. Having admitted my dependence on God, I generally turn to prayer. Mahatma Gandhi said, "Prayer is a daily admission of one's weakness."

Do not be far from me, for trouble is near and there is no one to help

PSALM 22:11

On the morning of 11 September 2001, nineteen hijackers took control of four commercial passenger jets flying out of airports on the east coast of the United States. Two of the aircraft were deliberately flown into the two main towers (the Twin Towers) of the World Trade Center in New York, with a third hitting the Pentagon in Virginia. The fourth plane never reached its intended target, crashing in Pennsylvania. It is believed that the passengers and crew overpowered the hijackers and took control of the plane. Nearly three thousand people lost their lives, including the nineteen hijackers. Following the attacks, the media reported a twenty per cent increase in church and synagogue attendance. As people tried to make sense of what had happened they came together and prayed, perhaps sharing the burden of their lack of understanding and grief with God. In times of uncertainty, people pray more. And, according to a recent report from the Thinktank, *Theos*, prayer is good for us, whether we believe our prayers "work" or not.

If pain and suffering has the effect of making us confess our dependence on God, and engage in prayer, then it can be seen as having a role in shaping our identity. There is a verse in Isaiah which reads, "See, I have refined you, but not like silver; I have tested you in the furnace of adversity" (Isaiah 48:10). Pain and suffering can help to shape our identity and show us what we are made of. This is something St Paul is also aware of, he writes in his letter to the Romans:

We also boast in our sufferings, knowing that suffering produces endurance, and endurance produces character, and character produces hope, and hope does not disappoint us, because God's love has been poured into our hearts through the Holy Spirit that has been given to us.

ROMANS 5:3-5

Illness disrupts our lives and impacts our identity, sometimes resulting in a loss of identity. The loss of identity can itself be a form of suffering for those living with chronic illness. Physical pain is not the only sort of suffering. There is also a loss of self – a crumbling of self-image, a restricted life, social isolation, a feeling that you are a burden to others. At the point of my diagnosis I can remember looking back and seeing everything the MS had taken away from me, looking into the future, nothing was certain. I can distinctly remember thinking: what will happen to me now? What will I do? Would anyone want to marry me? What about having children? My sense of self was disrupted for quite some time. It was probably only Sheila's reaction to me, some thirteen years later, which helped me to start putting my sense of self back together, and to start really caring for myself again. In the time between my diagnosis and having James, I had fought with the MS and tried to "beat" it through diet. I bought a book titled, "Eat to Beat MS", or something similar. I became fanatical about organic food and hemp seed oil, and the first thing I ate every morning was fruit. Much of this fell by the wayside when I had James. I was too busy caring for him to prepare myself fruit salad for breakfast. I was doing well if I'd managed to get myself a slice of toast before it was lunchtime. Now I became largely disengaged with the MS, and more contemptuous of it. When I met Sheila I re-evaluated, perhaps I am now moving towards some sort of acceptance. It is very difficult, because I don't look ill, so even I think I should be able to do everything that my friends and those around me can. But I can't. There comes a point where the fatigue is too much and I run out of energy. I am learning to say "no" to certain things and not feel guilty about not being able to do it all. I am trying to give myself a break, and work towards twenty minutes of exercise a day, and twenty minutes of rest each afternoon. It can be hard to squeeze that in between the work that I do and caring for the children, but I am making an effort. And I have been for the occasional massage, which helps considerably with the spasms in my legs, and which I need to make a more regular thing. I am no longer fighting, or in denial. But it has taken some time. Perhaps I am finally moving towards the development of a new and equally valid sense of self. I might not have been able to have an academic career, but I have written this book.

My MS is an experience through which I have learned new definitions of self, and given up previous ones. I have been lucky thus far, my symptoms and relapses have eased since I have had my children. In that sense, my suffering has eased. If I was in the middle of a relapse, could I have sat down to write this book? Probably not. I'd be too focused on getting better again and whatever I had to do to get through the day. But I am in a position right now, where I can see my suffering in the terms St Paul talks about. Because it has been thirteen years, I can look back and see my earlier episodes as a path on a journey to knowledge and self-discovery. Looking into the future, none of us has any certainty – except for our faith and the hope of a promise of a new life to come. The difference between me, and others not living with a chronic illness, is that I am aware that control is an illusion and nothing can be taken for granted, and they may not be. I know that things may take a turn for the worse, but I hope and pray that they won't. I also know that if things do get worse, there is a good chance they will also get better again. There is always hope.

But you, O Lord, do not be far away! O my help, come quickly to my aid!

PSALM 22:19

In her interview for *The Guardian* in 2007, Delta Goodrem talked about her treatment for cancer, saying that this was "tough… I looked in the mirror. My face had a green tinge. My hair was falling out. I had lost so much weight and I thought, I don't recognise this person. You know rationally you're the same person, but you look and feel so different" (29 April 2007). In fact, Delta's cancer transformed her. In May 2004, Delta told *The Australian Women's Weekly*, "I have this idea that people look at me and think that, aside from the short hair, I am the same person, the same Delta. It's as though they are just waiting for my hair to grow back and I will be the same again, as though nothing has happened. But you can't go through something like this and be the same person at the end. It's simply not possible." She told the magazine that she has always believed in God and that prayer gave her comfort. "I believe in faith. I believe in angels. I believe that perhaps God sent me this challenge for a reason so I can help other people." My MS has helped me to crystallise what I consider to be important. I don't have as much energy as my friends and family. And when you live with a lower than normal amount of energy, your priorities change. I have to think about what I really want out of each day. I love Christine Miserandino's Spoon Theory:

One day Christine's friend asked her what it was like living with Lupus. Christine handed her friend twelve spoons and asked her to describe the events of a typical day, taking a spoon from her friend for each activity. The spoons represented units of energy, Christine explained her energy needed rationing if she was to avoid running out before the end of the day. Christine also explained that it is possible to exceed her daily limit, but that means borrowing from the future, and may mean not having enough energy for tomorrow. Christine posted her essay *The Spoon Theory* on her website *But You Don't Look Sick*. It's a brilliant disability metaphor. I know I can't swim for much more than half an hour in the morning, or I will use up too many spoons and I'll run out of energy to complete the school run and make dinner. The spoons are relevant to other aspects of my life too. My MS has also made me reflect on what is really important, and what it is that I want to achieve.

"...you can't go through something like this and be the same person at the end."

Ultimately, what matters are our relationships, with each other and – as discussed in the previous chapter - with God. Suffering reveals what is in our hearts, and also helps us to find one another. On Thursday 7 July 2016, five police officers were killed, and seven other officers and two civilians were injured, during a racially motivated shooting in the United States in Dallas. The shooting came during a peaceful protest against the police killings of two black men in Louisiana and Minnesota. A twenty-five-year-old former army reserve and Afghanistan war veteran opened fire at the demonstration. Dallas police chief, David Brown, said that Micah Johnson said he was upset with white people and wanted to kill them, "especially white officers" (*The Irish Times*, Dallas Shootings: US shaken after racially motivated ambush, 9 July 2016). In his statement about the shootings, The Bishop of Dallas, Kevin Farrell, said, "All lives matter: black, white, Muslim, Christian, and Hindu. We are all children of God and all human life is precious." The Redemptorists published a prayer on 9 July 2016 on their *Bread 4 Today app*, titled *Let us wake up*:

Not just from the Sunday morning exhaustion,
from the wish for a few more drowsy minutes in bed.
Let us wake up to this world we live in: to its beauty and wonder,
and also to its tragedy and pain.
We must wake up to this reality: that not all in our world have
what we do, however much or little that is.
We must wake up to the idea that our wholeness, our lives,
are only as complete as the lives of those around us, of those we
are inextricably tied to in a great web of mutuality, of which all
of us are part.

We must stay awake, in the words of our friends and colleagues involved in Black Lives Matter, working every day for racial justice in our country.

Let us wake up, let us stay awake.

Amen.

CHRISTIAN SCHMIDT

St Paul talks about us collectively making up the body of Christ. He says in his letter to the Romans:

For as in one body we have many members, and not all the members have the same function, so we, who are many, are one body in Christ, and individually we are members of one another. We have gifts that differ according to the grace given to us: prophecy, in proportion to faith; ministry, in ministering; the teacher, in teaching; the exhorter, in exhortation; the giver, in generosity; the leader, in diligence; the compassionate, in cheerfulness.

ROMANS 12:4-9

As parts of Christ's body, we need to be alive to the needs of others and how we can show empathy and love. As I write this, another song is starting to play in my head, the chorus begins:

People help the people
And if you're homesick, give me your hand and I'll hold it.

SIMON ALDRED, PEOPLE HELP THE PEOPLE (2007)

The poor shall eat and be satisfied; those who seek him shall praise the Lord. May your hearts live forever!

PSALM 22:26

Suffering comes with the freedom to choose. But God hears us when we cry out, and suffers with us in our suffering. Christ was nailed to a cross for us and made suffering redemptive, turned it round for our good. In union with Christ's suffering, ours too can be redemptive. If we feel Christ's presence is lacking in our suffering, might that be because others who make up the body of Christ, are not serving Christ as they could? Why doesn't God stop evil and suffering? We are Christ's body on earth, why don't we intervene? As a lecturer in Education I have been asked by students how I can believe in a loving God, having completed a PhD about how the Holocaust is taught as a topic in school history.

Auschwitz-Birkenau was liberated by Soviet troops on 27 January 1945. Auschwitz was the largest concentration and extermination camp built by the Nazis. We cannot be certain how many people lost their lives there, but it is estimated that between one and one and a half million died in Auschwitz: over one million were Jewish, around seventy thousand were Poles and around twenty thousand were Gypsies. About fifteen thousand were soviet prisoners of war. Between ten and fifteen thousand prisoners from other ethnic backgrounds also died in Auschwitz. The majority of victims were gassed, but many died as a result of malnutrition or disease. In all nearly six million Jews were killed during the Holocaust, which was part of a vast operation of genocide encompassing millions of Gypsies, people with mental and physical needs, gay people, and political and religious prisoners. The Nazis came to power in 1933 with the blessing and support of the German Right, German industrialists and the German army. Parliament immediately passed an act granting Hitler dictatorial powers. He then began a reign of terror against his political opponents, Communists, socialists, radicals and trade unionists. The first German concentration camp had been set up at Dachau in March 1933, less than two months after Hitler came to power. From the start, the guards in these camps were brutal, with those interned there subject to hard labour, floggings and executions. But understanding Hitler simply in terms of him being an "evil psychopath" is not helpful, we need to understand him as a human being. We also need to understand the psyche of those living in the Third Reich, who supported and co-operated with Hitler as perpetrators, and as bystanders who watched events in Nazi Germany unfold and did nothing. God made us all with a capacity to do great things, good or evil. None of us is wholly one or the other, none of us is immune from carrying out wicked deeds. In 2010 film director Oliver Stone told the Television Critics Association, "We can't judge people as only "bad" or "good". [Hitler] is the product of a series of actions. It's cause and effect" (Ed Pilkington, "Hitler? A scapegoat. Stalin? I can empathise. Oliver Stone stirs up history", *The Guardian*, 10 January 2010). The cruel and murderous policies pursued by the National Socialists were carried out by normal people, ordinary men and women, not by demons and monsters. And not by God.

Raul Hilberg has spoken about drawing a line through history and paralleling the Holocaust with similar atrocities, so that we can understand what causes genocide, in the hopes of any further repeat of history. In an interview with Erna Paris, Raul Hilberg said:

Do we want one Rwanda after the other? You know, when a group of Tutsis sits around and watches a neighbouring village burn, when they say, "Well that's them, it's not going to happen to us", they are repeating the history of the Dutch Jews who, when they heard about the Holocaust in Poland, said, "This is the Netherlands; it can never happen here". They are also repeating the words of the Germans in 1096 when they heard what the crusaders were doing in France. It is staggering to draw that line through the centuries and look at the sameness of language. You have to say, "Wait a minute, what's going on? Should we not look at this? Of course we should".

ERNA PARIS, *LONG SHADOWS: TRUTH, LIES AND HISTORY*
(LONDON: BLOOMSBURY, 2002), 335

In these examples used by Raul Hilberg, identities became divisive. But we can look for forms of identity which include, rather than exclude others, and which bind us together. From a Christian point of view, we are all one body, made in the divine image and likeness. As already noted, Hugo Gryn has been asked where God was during the Holocaust. But, he says, the real question is, "Where was man?" I want to start to bring this chapter towards an end, with a very powerful quotation which is featured in John Pritchard's book Ten: *Why Christianity Makes Sense* (London: SPCK, 2014). In this quotation, Hugo describes what he experienced on Yom Kippur in 1944. He was at his place of work, having lied to the SS officers at Auschwitz about his age on the advice of another prisoner, who had muttered to him in Polish as he got off the cattle truck at Auschwitz, "You are nineteen and you have a trade." This was a lie that saved Hugo's life. He watched his younger brothers being led towards the gas chambers, crying. Hugo was born in 1930, so he was fourteen in 1944 when on this holy day, the Day of Atonement, he like many others, fasted. Hugo cleared a hiding space for himself among the stacks of insulation boards and spent most of the day there, not even emerging for the thin soup that was given out at midday:

I tried to remember as many of the prayers as I could and recited them, asking for God's forgiveness for promises made and not kept. But eventually I dissolved in crying. I must have sobbed for hours. Never before or since have I cried with such intensity and then I seemed to be granted a curious inner peace. Something of it is still with me.

I believe God was also crying. And I understood a bit of the revelation that is implicit in Auschwitz. It is about a man and his idols. God, the God of Abraham, could not abandon me, only I could abandon God. I would like you to understand that in that builder's yard on the Day of Atonement, I found God. But not the God I had childishly clung to. People sometimes ask me "Where was God in Auschwitz?' I believe that God was there himself – violated and blasphemed. The real question is 'Where was man in Auschwitz?'

JOHN PRITCHARD, *TEN: WHY CHRISTIANITY MAKES SENSE*
(LONDON: SPCK, 2014)

"Man", humanity, was lacking. Hugo, and his father, survived Auschwitz and were moved to a slave camp, Lieberose. They lived through that too, and they survived the infamous death march to Sachsenhausen. But Hugo's father died three days after they were liberated. During the death march to Berlin, Hugo told of how Germans came out of their homes to spit on them. What made German citizens do this?

What happened in Nazi Germany needs to be viewed in the context of what was happening in the rest of Europe at the same time. Anti-Semitism was rife in Europe, as we can see from literature at the time. Look, for example at D H Lawrence's description of Sir Clifford Chatterley in *Lady Chatterley's Lover*. Lawrence describes Clifford Chatterley as possessing "a cold spirit of vanity, that had no warm human contacts, and that was as corrupt as any low-born Jew in craving for prostitution to the bitch-goddess, Success" (D H Lawrence, *Lady Chatterley's Lover*, (London: Penguin, 1961), 74. Anti-Semitism, and the eugenic ideas which fuelled Hitler's policies, weren't confined to Nazi Germany. There was support for some of Hitler's policies among people in Britain. Nella Last, the housewife and mother who was portrayed by Victoria Wood in *Housewife 49* (ITV, 2006), wrote in her wartime diary that she was surprised to find herself in agreement with Hitler's policies on compulsory "euthanasia":

I never thought I'd admire anything that Hitler did, but today, when I read in the *Sunday Express* that he "painlessly gassed" some thousands of lunatics, I did so. I believe firmly in euthanasia in incurable cases, whether of cancer etc. or of mind disease. Far from being cruel, I think it's the reverse – and cruel in the extreme to *withhold* the "gift of sleep". If I ever get to the stage when I would be a burden or endless worry to anyone, I'd "start off on my own". Not in any spectacular way – just quietly, with the least possible fuss or bother – and count it no sin... I felt like an argument on the subject, and started off, but to my *intense* surprise, my husband agreed heartily, and went further. He said he thought every able-bodied nurse and doctor, and even "ordinary people", will have enough to do to succour and bring to health the mentally fit, and that all food and services should be reserved for the sick and wounded.

RICHARD BROAD (ED.) AND SUZIE FLEMING (ED.), *NELLA LAST'S WAR: THE SECOND WORLD WAR DIARIES OF "HOUSEWIFE, 49"* (LONDON: PROFILE BOOKS, 2006), 95-96

The eugenics movement was big in Europe and the United States in the early nineteenth century. In 1910, Winston Churchill, as Home Secretary, drafted a proposal to sterilise, or put in labour camps, 100,000 "degenerate British citizens". I find it quite frightening to read this following extract from a letter D H Lawrence wrote to his friend, Blanche Jennings, in 1908 about how he would like to deal with society's "outcasts":

If I had my way I would build a lethal chamber as big as the Crystal Palace, with a military band playing softly, and a Cinematograph working brightly; then I'd go out into the back streets and main streets and bring them in, all the sick, the halt and the maimed; and I would lead them gently, and they would smile me a weary thanks; and the band would softly bubble out the "Hallelujah Chorus".

J T BOULTON (ED.), *THE LETTERS OF D H LAWRENCE. VOLUME 1,* 1901-1913 (CAMBRIDGE: CAMBRIDGE UNIVERSITY PRESS, 1979), 81

I, and others with similar diagnoses, may be considered as the "sick and lame". In Britain, "compulsory euthanasia" and sterilisation programmes were never legalised. In fact it was the Catholic Church that helped to defeat plans for a voluntary sterilisation programme here. We all have a choice to make about who we want to be. When I am asked if there is just one lesson to be learned from the Holocaust, what it would be, my answer it is that it could have happened anywhere. The choice of whether or not to come out of our homes and spit on those who need our empathy and love, is within us. Hugo is right that God was dethroned in Nazi Germany. As Christians, we are defined by our faith in Jesus. We don't know who we are, without telling others who he is. If we don't want to be a victim of mistaken identity and appear to be a weed rather than the sheaf of wheat that we really are, then Christ needs to be at the centre of our lives.

God holds our identity, our very essence.

Chapter Four

God loves me and is merciful

You who live in the shelter of the Most High, who abide in the shadow of the Almighty, will say to the Lord, "My refuge and my fortress; my God, in whom I trust."

For he will deliver you from the snare of the fowler and from the deadly pestilence;

he will cover you with his pinions, and under his wings you will find refuge;

his faithfulness is a shield and buckler.

For he will command his angels concerning you to guard you in all your ways.

On their hands they will bear you up, so that you will not dash your foot against a stone.

PSALM 91:1-5, 11-13

Michael Joncas' beautiful song, *Eagle's Wings*, is based on Psalm 91. The refrain is particularly affecting:

And he will raise you up on eagle's wings,

Bear you on the breath of dawn,

Make you to shine like the sun,

And hold you in the palm of his hand.

This reminds me of Diane Warren's lyrics in her song, *Because You Loved Me* :

You were always there for me, the tender wind that carried me

The light in the dark shining your love into my life.

Diane's song, *Because You Loved Me*, could almost be our response to God in Psalm 91. God gives assurances of protection and we thank God for all the mercy and love shown to us. Just listen to the song, Celine Dion sings it very well.

This song, and Psalm 91, underline the point of this chapter, which is that God is with us every step we take. In fact, even more than that, God is holding us by the hand, and carrying us when we get too tired to keep walking.

When Edgar was ten weeks old he had bronchiolitis. I was quite frightened. Not three months on from a difficult birth and a myriad of health problems of my own, this felt too much, and I began to lose any sense of perspective. Edgar was hospitalised and was on a drip, wired up to a monitor, and inside an oxygen box. I couldn't pick him up. I did everything I could. I sang, I stroked him, I expressed milk for him. But he wouldn't stop crying. And neither could I. My husband was at home, looking after James, my mum was unwell with flu. I was on my own at the hospital with Edgar. And I didn't feel as though I could cope at all. As the tears ran silently down my cheeks, I was shouting inside, "God, why are you doing this to me? This isn't fair. I've had enough." I remember looking down at Edgar and wondering if he even knew I was there. He looked tired and hot and angry. And then I can recall thinking about whether God was as upset as me to see a loved one in pain. And I realised that God hadn't abandoned us, I was just too upset to acknowledge God's presence. But God was there. When I say that God holds us, I really mean that. And when I say "us" I mean all that we are. Being human is about our mind and body, but it is also about more than our physical self and our self-consciousness. God holds our identity, our very essence.

In the course of writing this book, I am beginning to see my MS as a way that God can transform my understanding, so that I can be the person I am supposed to be in Christ. Before I met Sheila, I think that I might have been lost in the rather joyless pursuit of being someone God never created me to be, at least at some points and in some areas of my life. Because, looking back, I can see that since my diagnosis I have been blessed with opportunities through which (I hope) I have served Christ where I am. Throughout the process of my diagnosis and during the times I have been unwell, I have never felt abandoned by God, or that God has wanted me to suffer. But more than that, since my conversation with Sheila, I can see that God has raised me up on eagle's wings, and held me in the palm of his hand. Scottish theologian, John Swinton says in his book, *Dementia: Living in the Memories of God* (Norwich: SCM Press, 2012), that well-being is defined by the presence of God, rather than the presence or absence of illness or distress.

You who live in the shelter of the Most High, who abide in the shadow of the Almighty, will say to the Lord, "My refuge and my fortress; my God in whom I trust"

PSALM 91:1-2

In a chapter which talks about illnesses which affect the body and brain, and how God supports us through these, it is worth just thinking for a moment about our bodies and what they are for. We tend to focus a significant amount of attention on our bodies. We think an awful lot about how we look, and how our bodies feel and function. Both the media and advertising are obsessed with body image. I worry about my weight. I try and make an effort with my hair and make-up, I think it is important to present myself well. But who am I actually trying to please? After all: "Vanity of vanities, says the Teacher, vanity of vanities! All is vanity" (Ecclesiastes 1:2). There is also a view that our bodies should keep going no matter what as we can see in advertisements for products like cold and flu remedies, which are designed and marketed so that we can keep working even if we are unwell. It is important to remember that even God rested on the seventh day. Our physical self is important, and we should care for our body. Our body is a gift from God. St Paul writes in his letter to the Romans: "I appeal to you therefore, brothers and sisters, by the mercies of God, to present your bodies as a living sacrifice, holy and acceptable to God, which is your spiritual worship" (Romans 12:1). In his first letter to the Corinthians, Paul talks about our bodies (1 Corinthians 6: 12-20). My favourite line is verse fifteen: "Do you not know that your bodies are members of Christ?" Looking after ourselves doesn't mean losing a few pounds or trying to look nicer. It isn't even about trying to live longer. It's a spiritual discipline, using what we have – ourselves – to make a positive difference in the world, for God. In the end it all comes down to Jesus' Parable of the

Rich Fool (Luke 12:16-21). The rich farmer congratulates himself on how much he has and what he has achieved for himself. He builds bigger and better barns in which to store his grain and goods and delights in his wealth, "But God said to him, "You fool! This very night your life is being demanded of you. And the things you have prepared, whose will they be?" So it is with those who store up treasures for themselves but are not rich towards God" (Luke 12:20-22).

We are more than just our bodies. More than blood and bone. More than DNA. At Canterbury Cathedral, suspended above the site of the first tomb of Archbishop Thomas Becket, is a 6ft sculpture by Antony Gormley. The piece, called *Transport*, is made from old iron nails, taken from the repaired roof of the Cathedral. Our bodies are our transport through life, and through which we pass. As Gormley has said: "We are all temporary inhabitants of a body. It is our house, instrument and medium. Through it, all impressions of the world come and from it all our acts, thoughts and feelings are communicated." Our acts, thoughts and feelings, these are perhaps the essence of who we are. But illness has an impact on this, and therefore a part in shaping who we are. Issues concerning our physical selves and our identity can be difficult, especially when it comes to neurological conditions, brain injuries and dementia. We tend to define who we are by what we think, how we talk, what we can do, and how productive or interactive we might be. But this becomes a problem if something happens, like an accident or diagnosis which impacts on the way we think or talk, or how productive and interactive we are able to be. What does this mean for our sense of selves? Are we, as Dietrich Bonhoeffer asks in his poem, someone else now? No, we are not. Our identity remains intact. Jesus himself provides a good example here.

Throughout the Gospels Jesus is enormously productive and interactive, until the point when he is betrayed and "handed over" by Judas. Then we see an increasingly reflective and passive Jesus. He no longer exercises the same control over his own life as he did before. Immediately before his betrayal and arrest, Jesus confesses his dependence on God, praying on the Mount of Olives, "Father, if you are willing, remove this cup from me; yet, not my will but yours be done" (Luke 22:42). Though no longer in control of his own destiny, Jesus remains confident of his own identity. When Pilate asks him, "Are you the King of the Jews?" He answered, "You say so" (Luke 23:3). Jesus doesn't feel the need to justify himself, or engage in any discussion about who he is. Jesus knows who he is, this is how he was able to do what he did.

Rooting our identity in Christ changes our lives. In *Porta Fidei*, the letter written by Pope Benedict XVI announcing the Year of Faith, he said that we should keep our gaze fixed on Jesus, because everything is sorted out in the mystery of the Incarnation. Indeed, look at the example of the Archbishop of Canterbury, Justin Welby, and his reaction to the news that the man he thought was his father, is not. Here we begin to see how rooting our identity in Christ impacts on our whole understanding of the world, and the way we choose to live our lives. For others, a revelation such as this, has been devastating. But Justin Welby's reaction was calm, there was no identity crisis. God held him, and his identity, "in the palm of his hand". We are assured, in Psalm 91, of God's protection. This is a psalm which offers strength and encouragement.

Because you have made the Lord your refuge, the Most High your dwelling place, no evil shall befall you, no scourge come near your tent

PSALM 91:9-10

St Dismas asks Jesus to "Remember me" (Luke 23:42). Not being able to remember is something many of us fear. It is something I fear. Even if my life becomes more restricted, I would like to think I would be able to continue to enjoy the company of my family and friends and our shared memories and interests. Life is valued by what we remember, and what we think other people remember about us. The number of people living with dementia is rising. It is expected to reach one million in the UK by 2021. Are we looking for and recognising Christ in those with dementia?

God told Moses: I am who I am (Exodus 3:14). We are made in the image of likeness of God. So, we are who we are. If my MS is part of me, does that make it part of God too? "Who do you say that I am?" Jesus asks his disciples (Matthew 16:15). That question takes on a different perspective when asked of Jesus by someone suffering from dementia, or another condition which affects memory. But there is an idea that there is no sort of human suffering in which God cannot be found. If we are made in the image and likeness of God, can our frailties and afflictions also be found in God? Peter Kevern says so. He says that on the cross, we see a "demented" Christ, and that if Jesus:

was truly human then it is very unlikely that his last minutes of life on the cross were lived in full self-awareness: the arrest, sleep deprivation, blindfolding, beating, humiliation and hanging for long hours in the sun would all have contributed to the profound disorientation.

PETER KEVERN, "SHARING THE MIND OF CHRIST: PRELIMINARY THOUGHTS ON DEMENTIA AND THE CROSS", NEW BLACKFRIARS, 91/1034 (JULY 2010), 416

Having experienced all that it means to be human, including dementia, Kevern argues that Christ is present in dementia. He also says that dementia has the potential to be grace-filled, and show us something of who God is, and what it means to know him. Kevern also points out our connections to the past and the future. People with dementia are still the same person they were before, their dementia forms part of their life story and identity.

Being diagnosed with dementia is worrying and upsetting for the person concerned, and for their family and friends. Kevern describes the enormous difficulty dementia presents to identity:

The personality of the individual may appear to change, sometimes dramatically; they may become more violent or sexually uninhibited. This "progressive neurological impairment" appears as an unstoppable leaking away of personhood, of identity and finally humanity: for this reason it is often referred to as a sort of "living death". What makes this particularly challenging for the committed observer is that the person seems to have lost whatever it is that makes them human, a sort of self-awareness or (to use an old term) "self-possession".

Kevern goes on to sum up the problem when he writes, "From the point of view of western society, dementia appears as a challenge to our assumptions of what makes a human being human" (Peter Kevern, "Sharing the mind of Christ: preliminary thoughts on dementia and the Cross", *New Blackfriars*, 91/1034, July 2010, 409). Where is God in dementia? As somebody's ability to relate to the world around them is diminished, and they become more isolated, it is also the case that their relationship with God can be strengthened and provide a source of comfort and support. Ben Bano is the producer of *It's still ME, Lord… A film exploring Spirituality and Dementia* (Caritas Social Action Network, 2009).

This DVD is about understanding and meeting the spiritual needs of people with dementia. Ben has said that sometimes when he has been ministering to a person with dementia, they have spontaneously prayed for him and his family, and suggested he needs to slow down and stop rushing around. Rather than being seen as "ministers" or "carers", we have an opportunity to become equal partners in a spiritual journey. Ben makes the point that understanding the spiritual needs of someone with dementia can promote dignity in the caring relationship, and says people with dementia are often particularly open to intense spiritual moments, living as they do in the present moment. But where is the "sufferer" in this? French philosopher René Descartes (1596-1650) said, "Cogito ergo sum", which is usually translated from the Latin into English as "I think therefore I am". What then, if you can no longer think, or your thoughts are muddled? Do you cease to be? I rather like Stephen G Post on this, he has suggested rejecting the notion of "I think therefore I am", replacing this "with the less arrogant notion 'I feel and relate, and therefore, I am'" (Stephen G Post, "Respectare: moral respect for the lives of the deeply forgetful", in Julian C Hughes, Stephen J Louw, Steven R Sabat (eds), *Dementia: mind, meaning and the person*, Oxford: Oxford University Press, 2006, 233).

In his book, Real Presences the philosopher George Steiner talks about identity and what makes us who we are. He says:

To learn by heart is to afford the text or music an in-dwelling clarity and life-force. Ben Johnson's term, "ingestion" is precisely right. What we know by heart becomes an agency in our consciousness, a "pacemaker" in the growth and vital complication of our identity.

GEORGE STEINER, *REAL PRESENCES*
(CHICAGO: THE UNIVERSITY OF CHICAGO PRESS, 1991), 9

This means that when we commit prayers, hymns, or passages from the Bible to memory they become, says Steiner, a very real part of us. Evidence in support of this idea can be seen in a remarkable example of validation therapy on *You Tube*. The clip shows Naomi Feil spending time with Gladys, who has dementia and is very withdrawn. Naomi sings hymns with Gladys which she obviously once committed to memory and which are very much a part of her. Naomi draws this part of Gladys out, helping her to re-member the songs she used to sing, and to feel happy and safe with Jesus.

As Rosalie Hudson puts it, in Christ we are "re-mented, re-minded, re-membered" (Rosalie Hudson, "Dementia and Personhood A Living Death or Alive in God?" *Colloquium*, 36/2, 2004 (2004), 137). Christ is present in the loneliness experienced by those whose lives are touched by a form of dementia. The full human integrity of those with advancing dementia is not diminished: they are still able to experience emotions both positive and negative, and share these with those who are able and willing to be present, as is seen in the very moving and powerful example of Naomi and Gladys. In this way, a person with dementia is seen not just as an object of care, but as a source of wisdom and experience. Person-centred care for those with advancing dementia is about focusing on that person and remembering who they are, remembering their humanity and dignity, as they continue on their pilgrimage - with an awareness of the continuing importance of their deeply held spirituality - and finding comfort in familiar prayers and rituals. At a conference organised by Ben Bano, Fr Daniel O'Leary said:

A spiritualty around dementia has to do with not denying people their humanness, their sense of identity, of being their own person. Friends and carers are called to be, in a sense, the memory for the person, to hold the fragments of a life together, a life to be seen, perhaps, in the light of past courageous enterprise and creative achievement. That intensely alive person, the glory of God as St Irenaeus put it, is still alive inside, though not always recognisable as such.

Daniel O'Leary, "The Hidden Grace of Dementia",
Welcome Me as I Am Website [online spirituality
and mental health resource], (8 October 2013)

We are the memory, we need to hold the fragments of the lives of those we care for in our hands, just like in the example in St Mark's Gospel where the faith of four others healed a paralytic man:

Then some people came, bringing to him a paralysed man, carried by four of them. And when they could not bring him to Jesus because of the crowd, they removed the roof above him; and after having dug through it, they let down the mat on which the paralytic lay. When Jesus saw their faith, he said to the paralytic, "Son, your sins are forgiven".

Mark 2:3-5

It is up to us to do the remembering for those around us who can't remember, or to have faith for those who are struggling to find theirs. The very beautiful line from Kathryn Greene-McCreight that I have quoted in the preface to this book, about us all being more than a collection of individuals, is preceded by this:

So when things seem entirely lost, and we give up on God, what do we do? Hopefully, and by the grace of God, we will remind ourselves that despite all appearances, God Is. God is with us. God is for us. We will help each other remember the identity of God: I AM WHO I AM.

Kathryn Greene-McCreight, *I Am With You*
(London: Bloomsbury, 2015), 97

When we help each other remember the identity of God, we help each other remember who we are too, and vice-versa. I've noted this in Chapter Three, and I'll come back to this again in the final chapter, but it is worth repeating: We are one in Christ.

Those who love me, I will deliver; I will protect those who know my name

PSALM 91:14

This is a thought-provoking verse given the discussion in this chapter about memory. What if we can't remember God's name? There are different ways of knowing. Different ways of loving, and whoever loves, knows God (1 John 4:7). Also, as just noted, we can know God not only individually but in relationship with others. This is because we are made in the image and likeness of a Trinitarian God. Our humanity – who we are – comes from our relationships and the communities to which we belong. Our lives are interrelated, interconnected and interdependent. St Augustine asks the Lord, "that I may know myself that I may know thee". Self-awareness is vital. There is a deep connection between self-awareness, other awareness and God-awareness.

In Chapter Two I talked about who Jesus is and his position in the Godhead. The Holy Spirit is mentioned throughout this book. What I haven't yet talked about is the Trinity. God exists as three distinct Persons: Father, Son and Holy Spirit. The Father is not the same Person as the Son; the Son is not the same Person as the Holy Spirit; and the Holy Spirit is not the same Person as the Father. They are three distinct Persons, but they are all one God. If we are going to understand what God is like, and how God relates to us and how we should relate to God, then we need to try and understand something about the Trinity. This isn't easy, in fact the doctrine of the Trinity is probably the most difficult to grapple with. I also find it utterly beautiful. It's the relationship between the three persons in the Godhead which is so interesting in terms of this book and that fundamental question of what makes us who we are. God is one essence and three persons, each person is fully God. Within God's one undivided being, there exist three personal distinctions, it is the relationship between these persons which makes God, God. It is our relationships which make us who we are.

There are those who become very angry with God when they, or someone they love, receives the diagnosis of a chronic illness. They are frightened and lose hope. None of us knows how we will react to certain things until we are faced with them. But I have friends whose faith I have watched grow and blossom in the face of the diagnosis of a terminal illness. For two in particular, their relationship with God entered a new phase. They bore out the words of Emmanuel Teney who said, "As your faith is strengthened you will find there is no longer the need to have a sense of control, that things will flow as they will, and that you will flow with them, to your great delight and benefit".

When David volunteered to fight against Goliath, he said, "The Lord, who saved me from the paw of the lion, and from the paw of the bear, will save me from the hand of this Philistine" (1 Samuel 17:37). David knew God had sustained him through dangerous situations in the past, as a result he had developed a fearless faith. Illness forces us to admit the fragility of life and confess our dependence on God. In St Matthew's Gospel there is an account of a father with a fearless faith: "'Lord," he said "have mercy on my son, for he is an epileptic and he suffers terribly; he often falls into the fire and often into the water"

(Matthew 17:15). This father is not meek and mild when he approaches Jesus, he is demanding, he highlights the failure of the disciples, "And I brought him to your disciples, but they could not cure him" (Matthew 17:16). This father demonstrates a complete conviction that Jesus can do what they could not. He confesses his dependence on Jesus.

In the end, perhaps knowing who we are isn't all that important. There is a difference between self-awareness, which is discussed in Chapter Six, and self-knowledge. Knowledge implies facts and information. But aren't these liable to change with interpretation? I used to teach a seminar about methods of educational enquiry to PhD students just embarking upon their research degrees. The Professor I taught with would use the example of historians Norman Gash and E P Thompson, each writing on the Peterloo Massacre, to assert that there is no such thing as "truth". The Peterloo Massacre of 16 August 1819 was the result of a cavalry charge into the crowd at a public meeting at St Peter's Field in Manchester. The meeting had been organised by the Manchester Patriotic Union Society, a political group which campaigned for parliamentary reform and the repeal of the Corn Laws, a price-fixing cartel which protected farmers' profits from cheap foreign imports, and kept bread prices high. A crowd of somewhere between thirty thousand and one hundred and fifty thousand people had gathered to hear Henry Hunt speak about the right to vote. What happened next is a matter of debate, but eleven people were killed, and several hundred were injured. Some of those killed were Waterloo veterans. The memory of the French Revolution and the fear of revolution spreading from Europe is likely to have influenced those in authority. Norman Gash sees Peterloo as a class war, E P Thompson as an administrative blunder. They have different interpretations of the facts. I don't believe that we as human beings can always know the truth about events (in this sense I agree with the Professor). But I do believe in the truth, which is not grasped as a thing, but is encountered in the person of Jesus. As long as he knows who we are and what we are worth, do we need to worry? Aren't we just navel gazing? I like Dietrich Bonhoeffer on this, and his poem Who am I? which ends:

Am I one person today and tomorrow another?
Am I both at once? A hypocrite before others.
And before myself a contemptible woebegone weakling?
Or is something within me still like a beaten army
Fleeing in disorder from victory already achieved?

Who am I? They mock me, these lonely questions of mine.
Whoever I am, Thou knowest, O God, I am thine!

What a beautiful last line.

Life is about love. We all matter because we all belong to the Creator of the universe.

God fills the hungry with good things

You cause the grass to grow for the cattle, and plants for people to use,
To bring forth food from the earth, and wine to gladden the human heart,
oil to make the face shine, and bread to strengthen the human heart.
The trees of the Lord are watered abundantly, the cedars of
Lebanon that he planted.

In them the birds build their nests; the stork has its home in the fir trees.
The high mountains are for the wild goats; the rocks are a refuge
for the coneys.

You have made the moon to mark the seasons; the sun knows its
time for setting.

You make darkness, and it is night, when all the animals of the
forest come creeping out.

The young lions roar for their prey, seeking their food from God.
When the sun rises, they withdraw and lie down in their dens.
People go out to their work and to their labour until the evening.
O Lord, how manifold are your works!
In wisdom you have made them all; the earth is full of your creatures.
Yonder is the sea, great and wide, creeping things innumerable are
there, living things both small and great.

PSALM 104:14-23, 24-26

In a 1996 interview for the *Los Angeles Times*, Joni Mitchell talked about her first trip to Hawaii, saying:

I took a taxi to the hotel and when I woke up the next morning, I threw back the curtains and saw these beautiful green mountains in the distance. Then, I looked down and there was a parking lot as far as the eye could see, and it broke my heart.

ROBERT HILBURN, "BOTH SIDES, LATER",
THE LOS ANGELES TIMES [ONLINE EDITION]
(8 DECEMBER 1996)

Joni sat down and wrote the song *Big Yellow Taxi* in which she uses that famous line, "they paved paradise and put up a parking lot". Joni's song is similarly concerned for its environmental concern. Pope Francis is similarly concerned for the environment. *Laudato Si* is Pope Francis' Encyclical on human ecology. In this letter, the Pope has called on us all to examine our hearts and think about how we care for our common home and all those who live here. The Pope quotes St Francis of Assisi in his opening line: *Laudato Si', mi' Signore*, which means, "Praise be to you, my Lord". Pope Francis reminds us of the words of St Francis in another song, St Francis' *Canticle of the Sun*. In this, St Francis conjures up the idea of a very intimate relationship with creation, as he talks about the universe being members of our own family. He refers to the sun, wind, air and fire as our brothers, and the moon, stars, earth, water and death as our sisters. I like the idea that our DNA is shared with all of creation:

Be praised, my Lord,
For all your creatures,
And first for brother sun,

Who makes the day bright and luminous.
He is beautiful and radiant
With great splendour
He is the image of you,
Most High.

Be praised, my Lord,
For sister moon and the stars.
You placed them in the sky,
So bright and twinkling.

In the first chapter of Genesis we see God create. We are appointed stewards of this creation: "The Lord God took the man and put him in the garden of Eden to till it and keep it" (Genesis 2:15). From the account of creation in Genesis, to the psalms, and right through to Jesus' parables, it is clear that the earth and everything upon it belong to God. As it says in Psalm 50, "For every wild animal of the forest is mine, the cattle on a thousand hills. I know all the birds of the air, and all that moves in the field is mine" (Psalm 50:10-11). The first verse of Psalm 24 is very specific: "The earth is the Lord's and all that is in it, the world, and those who live in it" (Psalm 24:1). We belong to God. We are told this over and over again: "Know that the Lord is God. It is he that made us, and we are his; we are his people and the sheep of his pasture" (Psalm 100:3). This is a fact which gives me a very profound reassurance of my self-worth, which is something that I struggle with, especially if I am feeling unwell. What use am I if I need to be cared for rather than providing care for others? But life is not actually about usefulness in this sense. Life is about love. We all matter because we all belong to the Creator of the universe. More than that, we don't just live on the earth, as St Francis says, and as it says in the first verse of Psalm 24, we are part of creation.

The diagnosis of a chronic illness can be like the moment the curtains are pulled back on life, and we see before us the mountains, the beauty of God's creation, and all that is truly important. There have been times when simply the ability to function has filled me with joy. Just opening my eyes, and being able to see a little bit more than I could the day before out of one or other of my eyes, as the optic neuritis subsides, is wonderful. On those days, watching the birds in the garden or the wind in the trees is utterly joyful. When I am unwell, all I want to do is be able to get outside. Since my diagnosis I have found pleasure and a sense of peace in simple, beautiful things: listening to birdsong, watching the blue tits playing in the garden or a robin hop along the fence. It is no wonder that at times when we are facing challenges, we have a greater desire to be closer to creation, because this is part of who and what we are. This chapter is about recognising ourselves as part of God's creation, it is about our own creativity and desire to create, and it is about how God uses creation to communicate with us.

Bless the Lord, O my soul. O Lord my God, you are very great
PSALM 104:1

I chose to start this chapter with Psalm 104 because this is a psalm which talks to me about nature's physical beauty and how this reflects God's glory. "I think God chose all the right colours," commented Edgar, looking out of the car window as we drove to school one morning. "The sky couldn't be anything but blue." It was the start of the new academic year and we hadn't done the school run for a while. I was pointing out the trees and how their leaves were beginning to change. "He couldn't make his mind up though, when it came to the trees, could he?" said James to Edgar. Quite true, I thought, during a few weeks in autumn we enjoy a display of various different colours: shades of red, yellow, purple, orange and brown. I like to make a woodland walk a feature of our October half-term activities. When the children were little we would take a plastic sandwich bag and collect leaves to make leaf-print pictures. The colours of the turning leaves are wonderful. Donovan wrote about colours, commenting just as Edgar had done, on the blue sky. (Donovan, *Colours*, 1965)

Perhaps one of the most striking things about life is that it has colour. In recent years there has been a significant growth in sales of adult colouring books. Sybil MacBeth has also written about praying in colour (*Praying in Color: Drawing a New Path to God* (Massachusetts: Paraclete Press, 2007). One review of this title noted, "Just as Julia Cameron, in *The Artist's Way*, showed the hardened Harvard businessman he had a creative artist lurking within, MacBeth makes it astonishingly clear that anyone with a box of colours and some paper can have a conversation with God" (Publisher's Weekly, 2007). Whenever we engage creatively with the world around us, we engage with God.

To see colour you have to have light. The sun's rays contain all the colours of the rainbow, mixed together. This mixture is known as white light. When white light strikes a white crayon, it appears white to us because it absorbs no colour and reflects all colour equally. A black crayon absorbs all colours equally and reflects none, so it looks black. Although artists consider black a colour, scientists don't, because black is the absence of colour. I think that's interesting, because from a theological point of view, you can also describe darkness, evil and hell as an absence of light and goodness, rather than entities that exist in their own right. Light sustains life, in fact it is the perfect orbit of the earth around the sun which sustains life. The connection between colour and light and life is something we allude to when we sing Sue McClellan, John Paculabo and Keith Ryecroft's hymn, *Colours of Day*:

Colours of day dawn into the mind

The sun has come up

the night is behind…

In this hymn, the light which reveals the colours of day is Jesus. When I told a friend about the conversation that I'd had with the children in the car, he commented that it revealed much about their ages. Edgar, who was almost seven, was young and innocent enough still to see the beauty of creation around him, but James at nine-and a half years, was starting to see death and decay. The beautiful coloured leaves that fall from the trees during the autumn are a symbol of this, much like over-ripe fruit and windfall apples. In Holman Hunt's famous painting *The Light of the World*, the apples on the ground are a symbol of desolation and decay. The apples have been discarded, perhaps this is a symbol of how some people treat Christ's invitation to get to know him. But the apples and the warm glow of the rather beautiful lantern that Jesus is holding in this painting, say something else to me. This painting says to me that it is autumn, and the nights are drawing in, we are losing light and the colours are changing, but despite the changing seasons, despite the inevitable death and decay, Christ remains: a constant source of light.

When you send forth your spirit, they are created; and you renew the face of the ground

PSALM 104: 30

In the sitcom, *Rev*, the character Reverend Adam Smallbone says, "In a way all art is an attempt at some level to describe creation. So you could argue, that it's always a religious act" (Tom Hollander and James Wood, *Rev*, Series 3, Episode 3, 2014). But the philosopher George Steiner says that art and the arts are even more than this. Steiner says that God is present, and speaks to us, through art and literature.

I have on occasion been asked by friends and students why God doesn't speak to us any more. If you read the Old Testament, God is pretty loquacious. The Bible records God speaking audibly numerous times. Bear in mind however, that the Old Testament represents thousands of years of history, so actually God might only have spoken aloud to us once every few thousand years. There is another point to bear in mind here too: there are other forms of communication. In his book, *Real Presences: Is There Anything in What We Say?*, George Steiner highlights the shortcomings of our use of language in authentic communication. He's quite right. Despite the fact most of us have a mobile phone, we don't in fact tend to communicate with our voices. We email and text, even when the person we are sending messages to is in the same building. When we Tweet, our messages are limited to one hundred and forty characters. Although we think we are communicating more, we are actually speaking and listening to each other less. The same can be true of relationships with God: too much talking and not enough silence. It's in the silence that I hear God, though not audibly.

What makes us human is our relationships, and when it comes to real emotion in relationships, whether it is pain or desire, silence often says more. As George Steiner has said, emotion resists communicative transfer into speech (George Steiner, *Real Presences* (The University of Chicago Press, 1991) 92). There are many different ways to communicate. The rock group Extreme sang about love being "more than words" on their 1990 album *Pornograffitti*:

Saying I love you

Is not the words I want to hear from you

It's not that I want you

Not to say, but if you only knew

How easy it would be to show me how you feel

More than words is all you have to do to make it real.

Nuno Bettencourt, who co-wrote the song, described it as a warning that the phrase "I love you" was becoming meaningless: "People use it so easily and so lightly that they think you can say that and fix everything, or that you can say that and everything's ok. Sometimes you have to do more and you have to show it – there's other ways to say 'I love you'" (Kira L Billik, "Extreme: Boston Group Riding the Funk-O-Metal Machine", *The Albany Herald*, (20 June 1991) 4B). For me, Jesus is proof of this.

Jesus showed his love by sacrificing himself for humanity, just as he said he would when he raised his friend Lazarus from the dead: "The sisters [of Lazarus: Mary and Martha] sent a message to Jesus, 'Lord, he whom you love is ill'. But when Jesus heard it, he said, 'This illness does not lead to death; rather it is for God's glory, so that the Son of God may be glorified through it'." (John 11:3-4). The "he" in this first piece of scripture could be substituted for "humanity" so that it would read, "Lord, *humanity* whom you love is ill...". Those who were there at the time did not really understand what Jesus was telling them: that by raising Lazarus from the dead, a sequence of events would be triggered that would result in the defeat of death for all humanity. God's greatest masterpiece of creation is us. It is you. And God's love for us is greater even than Matisse's love for his work in the Chapel of the Rosary at Vence (we'll come to this very shortly). God's own Son is sent to save from destruction the greatest artwork produced by our Creator.

I like Steiner's understanding of art. As I have said, Holman Hunt's painting *The Light of the World* says to me that God is with us always. And this is one of the things that Steiner talks about, narrative in aesthetic form, or in other words, pictures which "speak" to us:

Serious painting, music, literature or sculpture make palpable to us, as do no other means of communication, the unassuaged, unhoused instability and estrangement of our condition.

GEORGE STEINER, *REAL PRESENCES*
(THE UNIVERSITY OF CHICAGO PRESS, 1991), 139

I have witnessed my nephew engaging with the Easter story in a new way, after looking at a wood carving of one of the Stations of the Cross. "Aunty Lucy, that is really freaking me out!" said my nephew, wide eyed and recoiling in the church pew. I turned to where he was looking so intently, to see a wood carving of the eleventh station: Jesus is nailed to the cross. "It wasn't nice, what they did to Jesus, was it?" I said to him. "No", he replied, "that would really, really hurt." "I know, crucifixion was a horrible way to die. But remember if Jesus hadn't been crucified, he couldn't have risen from the dead and we wouldn't have Easter.

Jesus did that for us because he loves us so much." My nephew goes to a Catholic School and is familiar with the Easter story. He knows Jesus was nailed to a cross and was crucified, but the wood carving on the church wall spoke to him in a way that reading or listening to the Easter story had not. The artwork on the church wall was a conversation between my nephew and God, which deepened his understanding. Matter – wood, stone or metal – is for this reason, described by George Berkeley as one of "the languages of God" (George Steiner, *Real Presences* The University of Chicago Press, 1991), 16.

Pope John Paul II wrote to artists saying:

With loving regard, the divine Artist passes on to the human artist a spark of his own surpassing wisdom, calling him to share in his creative power. Obviously, this is a sharing which leaves intact the infinite distance between Creator and the creator, as Cardinal Nicholas of Cusa made clear: "Creative art, which is the soul's good fortune to entertain, is not to be identified with that essential art which is God himself, but is only a communication of it and share in it."

LETTER OF HIS HOLINESS POPE ST JOHN PAUL II TO ARTISTS, 1999

In fact the philosopher George Steiner says that the only reason poetry, music and art exist is because there is creation. Like God, artists are driven to create:

"God is in reality nothing but another artist" (otro artista) declared Picasso whose own appetite for invention, for self-recreation was, indeed, that of a demiurge. Having completed his paintings in the Chapel of the Rosary at Vence, Matisse ruled: "I did it for myself". "But you told me you were doing it for God", objected Sister Jacques-Marie. Matisse: "Yes, but I am God".

GEORGE STEINER, *REAL PRESENCES*
(THE UNIVERSITY OF CHICAGO PRESS, 1991), 209

Picasso and Matisse's jealous rivalry with God, tells us something about God's own desire to create and love for creation, as well as the creative genius of God. God is revealed through creation, and uses creation to draw us into a relationship. Since we are made in the image and likeness of God, there is a spark of divinity within each of us. The creative desire of artists like Picasso and Matisse is a mere reflection of God's creative desire. It's a desire which exists within us all to some extent. Picasso is widely quoted as having said that "Amateurs borrow and great artists steal" and the artist Grayson Perry has commented that "originality is very overrated." He says that art, music and culture evolve, and we are inspired by others (speaking on *The Chris Evans Breakfast Show*, BBC Radio 2, 14 September 2014).

May the glory of the Lord endure forever; may the Lord rejoice in his works

PSALM 104: 31

During his appearance on *The Chris Evans Breakfast Show*, Grayson Perry told Chris Evans that "we are what [has] happened to us" (*The Chris Evans Breakfast Show*, BBC Radio 2, 14 September 2014). There is a lyric in the song *Knowledge of Beauty* by Dexy's Midnight Runners: "If I need strength to take bad on, I just look back to where I came from". It is a lyric I used to have written up on a poster on my classroom wall when I taught history. Our history informs our present and our future. But C G Jung might take issue with this, Jung said, "We are not what has happened to us, we are what we wish to become." This is interesting from my point of view. I have MS. The process of that diagnosis happened to me. And I feel that it really did "happen" to me. I experienced a loss of dignity in those hospital rooms, being x-rayed, scanned, and poked and prodded while my reactions were tested. I felt that some of the doctors were more interested in my condition than they were in me. For a while I did become my "condition". I am coming around to the idea of my MS being a part of me, but it will never be all of me. In this sense, Perry and Jung are both right. I am in part my MS and my MS is in part me. Our experiences, and how we choose to respond to them, shape who we are. I am both what has happened to me, and what I wish to become. Henri Matisse actually provides a very good example of someone who was both what happened to him and what he wished to be.

In the last decade of his life, Matisse could no longer paint, but he retained his identity as a great artist despite becoming wheelchair bound. Lydia Delectorskaya, Matisse's studio assistant and secretary, recalls the starting point for his work *Oceania, The Sky*:

Matisse had cut out a swallow from a sheet of writing paper and, as it distressed him to tear up this beautiful shape and throw it away, he said, he put it up on his wall, also using it to cover up a stain, the sight of which disturbed him. Over the following weeks other shapes were cut out and put up on the same wall.

HENRI MATISSE: THE CUT OUTS: ROOM 4,
TATE [THE TATE GALLERY WEBSITE]

This was the beginning of the final chapter in Matisse's career, when unable to paint he began drawing with scissors. His ill health had led him to invent a new medium. In May 2014 I went to the Tate Modern to see the Cut-Outs exhibition. Reviewing the exhibition in *The Observer* Laura Cumming wrote:

That they [the cut-outs] were conjured with nothing more than paper, pins and scissors seems as extraordinary as the reduced circumstances in which they were made – by an old man unable to stand without support, often confined to a wheelchair and eventually to the penultimate resting place of bed.

By 1941 Matisse was in a wheelchair, following radical colon surgery aged seventy-one. He couldn't work at his easel any longer, "and yet became so creatively resurgent with the cut-outs that what he gratefully called his 'second life' could just as well apply to his work." For the last thirteen years of his life, paper and scissors gave Matisse colour and form, and allowed him to continue to express himself creatively, "This is what it took," says Laura Cumming, "not just the scissoring but the pinning, trying it all out over and over again until the relationships between the pieces are exactly right." That re-arranging of all the pieces until the relationship between them was right, defined the work Matisse produced. It's also how our own identity is defined, by working out our own relationships. Commending the exhibition to her readers, Laura notes that this is in fact "the lesson of a lifetime, and an inspiration to the viewer: this is how we should all be, still aspiring, still relishing the beauty of life even as we face its end" (Laura Cumming, "Henri Matisse: The Cut-Outs review – 'the lesson of a lifetime'", *The Observer*, 20 April 2014).

One of Matisse's cut-outs is called *The Parakeet and the Mermaid*. It's a mural of flowers with a parakeet hidden among the flowers on the left, and a mermaid on the right. "I had to make...this parakeet with coloured paper," said Matisse. "Well, I became a parakeet. And I found myself in the work" (The Musuem of Modern Art, "Henri Matisse The Cut Outs"). I often find myself in my writing. There are times when I sit down to write an article, without really knowing where the piece is going or where it will end up. I take inspiration from daily life and the world around me. Artwork, literature and nature, inspire us to respond creatively. Playing a musical instrument, painting, drawing, writing, gardening, knitting, sewing, cooking, all of these activities can be therapies which give us the mental space either to think, or not to think at all but just to be. Creative activities can distract from the pain and stress and – George Steiner would say about music, art and literature - inspire a religious experience.

Our hobbies help us to get in touch with our true selves. You could say that my MS has made me more creative, because this ensured I stayed at home with the children, where I have done all sorts of things and experienced numerous moments of joy that I wouldn't otherwise have done. Those experiences and joys have formed the basis of much of my writing, which I have nurtured far more since my diagnosis. I know that I am lucky to have been able to continue to write. Sometimes much loved pastimes have to be given up, but here there is an opportunity to find something new, as in the example of Henri Matisse. Chronic illness can impact on our hobbies in other ways too. There is a danger that a diagnosis can take over our whole life. I was determined to have something for and of myself, and I have maintained my identity as a writer. If I had let my MS take up all of my focus, my sense of identity would have been lost. If I hadn't been diagnosed with MS, I would have continued to pursue an academic career when I had my children. When I told one of the professors I worked with that I wasn't planning to return to work after I had had my baby, she was surprised, "But children grow up and leave home, and then what will you have left?" There is a point here. If you speak to anyone whose children have recently left home, questions about identity and a sense of purpose often come up, although this is true whether they have a professional career or not. Those who have recently retired also ask themselves questions about who they are as well as how they will fill their time. It won't be long before James goes to secondary school, and it only seems like five minutes since he was at nursery school. I quite often wish I could press "pause" on life for just for a little while, to take a breath. I recently found a very good prayer for that time when the children leave home and for when retirement comes along:

How brief life seems. The children have flown the nest and made nests of their own.

Mum and Dad have passed on. And I find myself in the middle of a life barely remembered and passed, and a life hard to imagine and ever approaching.

Perhaps, Lord, it would be good to enjoy the present, grateful for the past and hopeful about the future.

O Mystery, ever ancient ever new, as you embrace creation today, enjoy us enjoying all you have given us. Amen.

This is a prayer which was published on the Redemptorist's *Bread 4 Today* app on 15 September 2016. What a poetic last line, "enjoy us enjoying all you have given us", I think this means creation itself and the brothers and sisters St Francis talks about, as well as the families and relationships we have helped to create, and the opportunities which are given to us to work to support our families. It is a very lovely prayer, and acting it out and enjoying our lives must surely be an even more beautiful prayer to God. Because, having given someone a present, what is nicer than watching their face as they unwrap it with wonder and delight, and see them go on to enjoy the gift. Our lives are God's gift to us, the way we live them is our gift to God.

While retirement can take some getting used to, I find it hard to believe that anyone gets to the end of their life and wishes that they had worked more. We shouldn't live to work, we should work to live. For parents who have decided to stay at home to look after their children, there is a danger of living through them, trying to push them in directions that we wished we had gone rather than the way they want to go. But this is something I am very wary about. In 2011, I had the opportunity to have a written conversation with Rachel Denton, who lives in Lincolnshire as a hermit. This conversation was published in the Redemptorist Sunday news sheet, *Sunday Plus*. As I said to Rachel in the course of that conversation, forays back into academic life as a Visiting Tutor after I had had James, both sustained and confused me. I wrote to Rachel about being asked, during dinner with friends, whether I considered my PhD or my children to be my greatest achievement. The assembled company were of the view that the answer should be my children, I wasn't so sure. I am proud of James and Edgar. I hope that I am doing a good job as a mother, but what I want for them is to be happy and independent. I try to support and encourage their own gifts and talents without pushing things I wish I had done but didn't. Having said that, I am aware I am not a perfect parent. Can any parent be perfect? The poet Philip Larkin wouldn't say so, just read his poem, *This Be The Verse*. There will come a point when I will need to let go, and let James and Edgar make their own way in the world. But I am glad to have had the opportunity to be at home with them. Beyond the daily grind, it has proved to be a very creative time.

I will sing to the Lord as long as I live; I will sing praise to my God while I have being

PSALM 104:33

All of creation speaks of God's glory, including aspects of creation which are not valued culturally. There is an aspect of creation that I particularly want to consider before the end of this chapter, and that is vulnerability as a creative part of human living. As discussed in Chapter Three, we don't understand why there is suffering in the world, but we know that not even Christ was spared this. We were never promised that our suffering would be taken away, but Christ walks our way of the cross with us, as we walk with him. During Pope St John Paul II's visit to the United Kingdom in 1982, he spoke at Southwark Cathedral:

I want you to know how I have looked forward to this meeting with you, especially with those of you who are sick, disabled or infirm. I myself have had a share in suffering and I have known the physical weakness that comes with injury and sickness. It is precisely because I have experienced suffering that I am able to affirm with ever greater conviction what Saint Paul says: "Neither death, nor life, nor angels, nor principalities, nor things present, nor things to come, nor powers, nor height, nor depth, nor anything else in all creation, will be able to separate us from the love of God in Christ Jesus our Lord".

ROMANS 8:38-39

It is worth thinking about the words of Pope St John Paul II in the light of the life of St Bernadette, who is the Patron Saint of Illness. Bernadette was born in Lourdes on 7 January 1844. Her parents were poor. Bernadette had little education and couldn't read or write. As a toddler, she contracted cholera. She also suffered from asthma and so she lived all her life in poor health. Bernadette died aged just thirty-five.

Our Lady first appeared to Bernadette while she was out collecting firewood with her younger sister and a friend. Bernadette was fourteen. There followed a series of visions there, eighteen in total, which led to the founding of Lourdes as a place of pilgrimage. Between the eighth and twelfth apparitions, Bernadette does some very strange things. She gets down on her knees; she kisses the dirty ground; she eats some bitter grass; she scrapes around trying to drink the muddy water; she puts mud on her face. What is she doing? She does what she is asked to do by Our Lady. And the site where she gets on her knees in the mud is the place where Bernadette's spring starts to flow, it is still flowing at a rate of thirty-two thousand gallons a day. There are two things in particular I find noteworthy about Bernadette's scraping about in the mud. One is her physical closeness to nature and creation. She quite literally communes with nature, smearing mud on her face and consuming grass and muddy water. The second thing is that by the time she was doing this, Bernadette had an audience of local people who followed her to the grotto. They thought she was mad. They couldn't see Our Lady, and no-one, not even Bernadette, had any idea what she was doing. She simply did as Our Lady asked her. This is surely a metaphor for God's presence with us. God comes to us where we are. Is there with us in the mud, inviting us to be one with creation. We don't usually achieve enlightenment, but we are in the real presence. Today Lourdes is the most visited Christian shrine in the world, receiving between four and six million pilgrims each year, many of whom are sick and hoping to be healed. They bathe in pools of water from Bernadette's spring.

St Bernadette's attitude to her own suffering is thought-provoking. From 1866 to 1879 Bernadette lived a religious life in a convent in Nevers. As Sister Marie Bernard, she lived the simple life of a nun, avoiding the fame and attention that would have otherwise been a part of her life. During her time as a nun, Bernadette frequently suffered from ill-health, but her humility, obedience and cheerful attitude meant that young novices gained inspiration from spending time with her. In the convent Bernadette said, "I am getting on with my job." Asked what her job was, she replied, "Living as somebody who is ill". She prayed, "Lord, I do not ask that I never be afflicted, but only that you never abandon me in affliction". It is a beautiful prayer, which runs counter to "Why me? What have I done to deserve this?" In fact, in his address in May 1982 at Southwark Cathedral, Pope St John Paul II said, "Sickness and suffering seem to contradict all that is worthy, all that is desired by man." He went on, "*And yet no disease, no injury, no infirmity can ever deprive you of your dignity as children of God, as brothers and sisters of Jesus Christ*". We all of us face challenges of one kind or another:

Today I make an urgent plea to this nation. Do not neglect your sick and elderly. Do not turn away from the handicapped and the dying. Do not push them to the margins of society. For, if you do, you will fail to understand that they represent an important truth. The sick, the elderly, the handicapped and the dying teach us that weakness is a creative part of human living, and that suffering can be embraced with no loss of dignity. Without the presence of these people in your midst you might be tempted to think of health, strength and power as the only important values to be pursued in life. *But the wisdom of Christ and the power of Christ are to be seen in the weakness of those who share his sufferings.*

POPE ST JOHN PAUL II, SOUTHWARK
CATHEDRAL (MAY 1982)

As reflected on in Chapter Three, evil cannot be seen as a part of creation. But our response to our own suffering, as well as to the suffering of those around us, can be understood as something which makes us human. Or in other words, suffering draws out our humanity. In October 2016 the BBC broadcast a documentary in which the comedy actress, Sally Phillips, talked about Down's Syndrome and the kind of society we all want to live in ("A world without Down's Syndrome?", *Dragonfly Film and Television for BBC 2*, 5 October 2016). The programme highlighted some very disturbing truths, including the fact that nine out of ten women in the UK who are told their baby has Down's Syndrome, choose to terminate their pregnancy. In Iceland, one hundred per cent of mothers who are told their baby has Down's Syndrome choose a termination. This prompts Sally to ask in her commentary, "Why is Down's Syndrome the disability that it's socially acceptable to terminate, and how do we come back from that?" It's a question that reminded me of Pastor Martin Niemoller's poem, *First They Came*:

First they came for the Communists

And I did not speak out

Because I was not a Communist

Then they came for the Socialists

And I did not speak out

Because I was not a Socialist

Then they came for the trade unionists

And I did not speak out

Because I was not a trade unionist

Then they came for the Jews

And I did not speak out

Because I was not a Jew

Then they came for me

And there was no one left

To speak out for me.

With prenatal screening and DNA sequencing becoming more and more reliable and available, who is to say which group of people will be screened out next? Sally's concluding comments are thought-provoking:

If we are heading towards a world where we choose more and more who gets born, I feel like we really need to think about what it is that we value. And as our powers of choice get greater and greater, who are those people that society might leave behind? There is great value in things not being perfect. There is a crack in everything, that's how the light gets in. And the imperfections are where humanity is most visible.

Sally took the words right out of my mouth. I wrote the next sentence months before her documentary was broadcast: It is in being present with our vulnerability that our deepest humanity is revealed. And it is in this way, my MS has had an impact on my identity and has made me more empathetic to others. As I continue through life and along my own journey of faith, I feel as though I am becoming more and more myself.

Our lives are about our journey to our heavenly home.

Chapter Six

God lifts up the lowly

I give you thanks, O Lord, with my whole heart; before the gods
I sing your praise;

I bow down toward your holy temple and give thanks to your name
for your steadfast love and faithfulness; you have exalted your name
and your word above everything.

On the day I called, you answered me, and increased my strength of soul.

All the kings of the earth shall praise you, O Lord, for they have heard
the words of your mouth.

They shall sing of the ways of the Lord, for great is the glory of the Lord.

For the Lord is high, he regards the lowly; but the haughty he
perceives from far away.

Though I walk in the midst of trouble, you preserve me against
the wrath of my enemies;

you stretch out your hand, and your right hand delivers me.

The Lord will fulfil his purpose for me; your steadfast love,
O Lord, endures forever.

Do not forsake the work of your hands.

PSALM 138

In St Paul's letter to the Ephesians he wrote: "For we are what he has made us, created in Christ Jesus for good works, which God prepared beforehand to be our way of life" (2:10). God has a plan, and in Christ, we get the chance to discover ourselves and work with God to refine our own characters. We are all searching, looking for our homeland. Abraham looked forward to a city founded, designed and built by God. We desire "a better country, that is, a heavenly one" (Hebrews 11:16). Our lives are about our journey to our heavenly home. I am not the same person I was ten years ago, and that person was not the same as the person ten years before that. This chapter looks at our identity as an ongoing process. Life is an adventure, and how we live it matters. There is a purpose to everyone's life, although we might never know what it is.

Shortly after he became Pope, Benedict XVI said, "Each of us is willed, each of us is loved, each of us is necessary." When Pope Francis visited the Greek island of Lesbos to meet migrants in April 2016, he took three Syrian families with him on the papal plane back to the Vatican. The Pope described his actions as a "humanitarian gesture…[but] a drop in the ocean." That may well be true, but the thing is that by adding a drop to the ocean, the whole ocean is changed ontologically. We have the power to change ourselves and our own lives, and the power to change the people around us and their lives too.

On the day I called, you answered me, you increased my strength of soul

Psalm 138: 3

There are various interpretations of Annie Lennox and David Stewart's song *I Saved The World Today*. One of the interpretations I have come across suggests that this song is about looking after yourself and not worrying about anyone else, because you can't solve the world's problems by yourself. With the advent of twenty-four hour news, the Internet, social media and smart phones, the world has become a smaller place. News alerts ping onto my phone-screen day and night, and the problems and sadness of the world can feel overwhelming. It is true that individually we can't make it all better however much we would like to. But that shouldn't stop us from trying or from caring.

When in the summer of 2016 it was reported that neighbours of an elderly couple in Italy had overheard crying, the police went to investigate. Eighty-four-year-old Jole, and ninety-four-year-old Michele, told the police that they were desperately saddened by the state of the world. The couple hadn't been visited by anyone for months. They explained to the police that Jole had become overwhelmed by stories of abuse and war on the television, and had begun to cry desperately. Her partner became despairing at her grief, and started to cry too. The police officers who visited them spent some time with the couple, asked if they could go into the pantry, and cooked them pasta and parmesan. In a statement the Rome police said, "Sometimes the loneliness melts into tears. Sometimes it's like a summer storm. It comes suddenly and overtakes one." The police couldn't solve the problems and sadness which is endlessly reported on the television news. But what they did was give Jole and Michele some reassurance, and perhaps restore some of their faith in humanity.

No-one can change the world by themselves, but everyone, whatever their circumstances and no matter how small, can do something. It might be a charitable contribution, it might be making a bowl of pasta and spending some time with someone, or it might be just smiling and saying "good morning". The smallest things can make the biggest difference to all our lives.

I remember James being off from pre-school with chickenpox. Despite being covered with spots he was otherwise well, which made the week rather a challenge. He wanted to do things, like go swimming, which he obviously couldn't. So I spent much of the week organising and clearing up seemingly endless activities like painting, cutting and sticking, playing cafés, making cakes, and I'm not sure what else. By about Wednesday I was thinking of changing my name as James called, "Mummy, can I have...", "Mummy, come and look at this...", "Mummy, could you just...", "Mummy, can we play..." I patiently and lovingly attempted to meet all of his constant and endless demands, while craving just half-an-hour to have a cup of tea in peace. Although I kept smiling outwardly, I was inwardly whimpering, "Please leave me alone for a minute...". Which made me begin to wonder how God feels? Made in the image and likeness of God, does God share our temperament and crave just a few minutes off? I don't think so.

St Paul wrote in his letter to the Philippians, "Do not worry about anything, but in everything by prayer and supplication with thanksgiving let your requests be made known to God" (Philippians 4:6). "Lucy, it's not a shopping list," a friend once said to me about my prayers. I remarked on this to another good friend some years later. "Of course it's a shopping list," he replied. "And what's more, you should get a supermarket style loyalty card so you can claim more rewards the more you pray!" We are encouraged to take our problems to God, not only by St Paul, but also by St Peter: "Cast all your anxiety on him, because he cares for you" (1 Peter 5:7). Perhaps the key words from the first of these two quotations are "supplication with thanksgiving". One very refreshing thing about the week James had chickenpox was when we went to feed the ducks and see the ducklings, and he said, "Thank you, Mummy that was fun". It's always nice when the children remember to say "thank you" without prompting. And I have always been much more inclined to accommodate their requests when they are polite and positive (though I do try and meet them even when they aren't). I wonder how different God is in this regard. My good friend has a point. We do get rewards the more we pray, but of course prayer isn't just about asking for things. It is also about saying thank you, and just spending some time with God doing something nice. But the point is, that even if all we can do is pray about the world's problems and our own problems, then that is something that we can do proactively. And small things, like just smiling, saying thank you, and acknowledging what someone else is going through, really do make a difference.

Though I walk in the midst of trouble, you preserve me against the wrath of my enemies

Psalm 138:7A

There are also other interpretations of *I Saved The World Today*. Some would say the song is about depressive illness, and that it talks about serious depression which prevents the sufferer from thinking about the needs of anybody else. This is the sort of depression which means that even though the person who is suffering knows that they are not starving, and there is no obvious cause for their depression, they can't lift themselves out of it.

Even if this song is about depression, the point I want to make in this chapter is that we all have something to offer, and we are all invited by God to fulfil a special purpose, despite any depression or chronic illness. We are not God, we cannot solve the problems of the world, but we can all make a difference. The type of people we become is more important than any of our successes or failures in the world.

In his book on the *Stations of the Cross*, Fr Timothy Radcliffe reflects on daring to look at ourselves with honesty in his meditation on the third station, Jesus falls for the First Time:

First falls are marked by shame and denial. They shake our self-image. After eating the fruit, Adam blames it on Eve: "The woman whom [you gave] to be with me, she gave me the fruit of the tree, and I ate" (Genesis 3:12). Eve also passes the buck: "The serpent beguiled me, and I ate" (v.13). So it's God's fault, or that other person or the serpent.

TIMOTHY RADCLIFFE, *STATIONS OF THE CROSS*,
(LONDON: BLOOMSBURY, 2015), 21-22

Fr Timothy goes on to write, we think "But it cannot be me. I am not like that" but in fact, "we are indeed just that sort of person" (Timothy Radcliffe, *Stations of the Cross* (London: Bloomsbury, 2015), 22). Eve and Adam could both have said, "No, thank you". But they didn't. Fr Timothy says that rather than remaining mired in shame or fear after we have fallen, we need to summon up a sense of wonder and adventure. We have the power to re-craft ourselves along the way. Even if we generally make good choices, that isn't to say we always will or do. But we have free choice, which means we have the ability to change who we are.

So rather than eating the fruit we have been asked to stay away from, how do we lead a fruitful life? The most fruitful, loving and happy life possible, has to be one that is fused with Jesus. Hours from his death, Jesus uses the short amount of time he has left to talk to his disciples and tell them:

Abide in me as I abide in you. Just as the branch cannot bear fruit by itself unless it abides in the vine, neither can you unless you abide in me. I am the vine, you are the branches. Those who abide in me and I in them bear much fruit.

JOHN 15:4-5

Jesus tells the disciples to remain in him. If I want to lead a fruitful life, then I have to remain in him. This is a relationship of deep, transforming intimacy. Like any relationship, it is perhaps not always easy. I have an aunt with MS. Her symptoms are different from mine and her diagnosis is more recent than my own. When she read the synopsis of this book I was pleased she was supportive, because I had feared that she would not like it at all. It has taken me a long time to get to this point, and to stop hating my MS and begin to see it as part of myself rather than as something which is attacking me. It's true that my aunt doesn't feel that the MS is a part of her. Where I am now, is not an easy place to get to. And I'm not suggesting that it is a place everyone will want to come to either. I'm not even sure it is a place where I would choose to be, or where I am utterly secure. What I am trying to do, in the light of my conversation with Sheila, is re-think myself. I am re-crafting myself. This has less to do with my MS and more to do with the fact that my MS and that conversation with Sheila, led me to a place where I am thinking about what makes me me, and who I want to be. My MS has prompted me to have a conversation with myself about where I centre myself. And regardless of the MS or anything else, I am convinced that where I want to root myself is in Jesus. This means not only believing in him and knowing him as the Son of the living God, it also means trying to become like him.

Richard Wurmbrand's life and actions provide a fantastic example of someone who managed to achieve this. He was born into a Jewish family in 1909 in Bucharest, Romania. Richard grew up to become an evangelical minister, converting to Christianity in 1938. His determination to spread the word of God meant that he spent fourteen years in prison, tortured by the communist authorities. When I read about Richard's treatment, I realise just how blessed

I am. Despite the torture and cruelty he endured, Richard kept his sanity and his faith. In fact, it was probably his faith that kept him together. He spent three years in solitary confinement in a cell twelve feet underground with no light. There was no sound, the guards even wore felt on the soles of their shoes. But Richard maintained his identity by composing and delivering a sermon each night in his cell. Because of his extraordinary memory, he was able to recall more than three hundred and fifty of his sermons, which he included in his book *With God in Solitary Confinement* (Oklahoma: Living Sacrifice Book Company, 1979). Richard communicated with other prisoners in neighbouring cells using Morse code. In this way, he continued to be the "light" to those people, rather than dwelling on the lack of physical light. Richard is an example of the fact that our relationship with God remains intact however dire the circumstances we find ourselves in. We can always invest in, and take something from that relationship. Richard did both from an underground cell where he was held in solitary confinement. When we show love to others and offer them hope, we do that for God. Richard's writing is wonderful. There are some beautiful and thought-provoking passages in *Tortured for Christ:*

Later, the Communists who had tortured us were sent to prison, too. Under communism, Communists, and even Communist rulers, are put in prison almost as often as their adversaries. Now the tortured and the torturer were in the same cell. And while the non-Christians showed hatred toward their former inquisitors and beat them, Christians took their defence, even at the risk of being beaten themselves and accused of being accomplices with communism. I have seen Christians give away their last slice of bread (we were given one slice a week) and the medicine that could save their lives to a sick Communist torturer, who was now a fellow prisoner.

RICHARD WURMBRAND, *TORTURED FOR CHRIST* (LONDON: HODDER & STOUGHTON, 2005), 59-60

As Richard writes, in the end, "God will judge us not according to how much we endured, but how much we could love" (Richard Wurmbrand *Tortured for Christ* (London: Hodder & Stoughton, 2005), 38). One of the more well-known sayings of St John of the Cross is. "At the end of our life, we shall be judged on our love".

You stretch out your hand, and your right hand delivers me

PSALM 138:7B

As is noted in Chapter Three, one of the explanations for suffering in the world is our free will. God has a plan for us, but we have the choice of whether we go along with that plan, or go our own way. C S Lewis explores themes of faith, free will and forgiveness in *The Lion, The Witch and the Wardrobe*. This is a book which has long been understood as an allegory of the Christian story. It is a story about faith, and the decision to follow Christ.

Having safely returned from tea with Mr Tumnus, Lucy could have decided not to go back to Narnia. While Narnia presented an alternative to life as an evacuee in wartime Britain, there were also elements to life in Narnia which were uncertain: the country was under an enchantment, it was always winter and never Christmas. Aslan obviously has a plan for the four Pevensie children. They have the opportunity to be Kings and Queens of Narnia. But it's very much a choice. Lucy (I am named after her,) ridiculed for her story about Narnia and Mr Tumnus, could have decided that she didn't want to get involved, but she is keen to go back and visit her new friend. Is he alright, or has the White Witch discovered that he gave Lucy up? Lucy is drawn through the wardrobe door, the door of faith. Edmund follows her, but meets the White Witch and chooses a different path. He will betray his brother and sisters. Lucy's faith is remarkable, she immediately accepts the truth and never veers from the path laid down for her by Aslan. She could perhaps be compared to one of the first apostles, leading the way for others. Peter and Susan initially lack conviction, but they follow Lucy and fulfil their purpose. Edmund's journey is more complicated, but his faith is ultimately just as strong as Lucy's. Perhaps the point here is that we all find a way through the door at different times and in different states of mind.

Edmund has, for me, got to be the most interesting character in this story. His own journey through Narnia is an exploration of betrayal and forgiveness. In the first part of the book, Edmund is a rather spiteful and difficult character who has no empathy for anyone. He seems angry, and well he might be. His father has presumably left for war, and he has been sent away from his mother and his home into the country to a place he doesn't know. His older brother and sister now take on a parental role, which he resents. So is it any wonder that he betrays his brother and sisters to the White Witch? As is noted in Chapter Five (of my book), Grayson Perry has said, "We are what [has] happened to us". Edmund makes some choices which are ill-judged because he is angry and probably frightened. But he is not a bad person, although it's not until Chapter Eleven of C S Lewis' story, when Edmund sees the Witch about to turn a group of creatures enjoying a Christmas party into stone, that his true self is revealed. The Witch strikes him for standing up for the party, and Lewis writes, "For the first time in this story [Edmund] felt sorry for someone besides himself." This is the beginning of a transformation in Edmund's character.

Edmund's actions will cost Aslan his life, at least initially. When Edmund is rescued from the Witch, he comes to meet Aslan, and they walk and talk together. This is a conversation which takes place in the "internal forum". Lewis doesn't record the exchange between the two. No-one overhears what Aslan is saying, all that is shared with the reader is the fact that this was a private conversation that Edmund never forgot. When Aslan then walks Edmund back to his brother and sisters, he tells them "there is no need to talk to him about what is past". Aslan ransoms himself for Edmund. What Aslan does is treat Edmund with love and acceptance. Edmund responds to this. Knowing how much he is worth to Aslan, makes Edmund a better person.

We participate in choosing our identity. Edmund made a choice to be loyal to the White Witch. Later, regretting that decision, he turns to Aslan. Edmund's decisions, actions and identity are formed by the events that happen to him, and his own interpretation of those events. We remember and re-member things which have happened to us. For some, perhaps suffering with post-traumatic stress, it is necessary to re-member and re-create a different history in order to live in the present. Identity is fluid, always developing, even in those who wish to fix their identity in place. Identity is a struggle between life's events, our interpretation of them, and our own will and action. The point of this chapter is to emphasise the "action" part of this equation. Because even if we choose to root ourselves in Christ and try to become more like him, that isn't the end. It is the beginning. Like any relationship, a relationship with God is a journey. Relationships involve input, and they grow and change.

Part of what makes us who we are is our faith, which can be defined as our relationship with God. Faith is about both how we relate to God, and how God responds to us. Jesus is introduced to a woman who has been caught in adultery. "Now in the law Moses commanded us to stone such women. Now what do you say?" Jesus is calm and collected. He bends down and writes on the ground. The people don't give up their questioning, pushing Jesus for an answer, so he straightens up and says to them, "Let anyone among you who is without sin be the first to throw a stone at her." Then he bends down again and carries on writing on the ground. When he looks up and sees those who condemned her have all disappeared, he says, "Woman, where are they? Has no one condemned you? ...Neither do I condemn you. Go your way, and from now on do not sin again" (John 8:5-11). Jesus doesn't give this woman a hard time. He isn't scandalised by her. He just tells her to make a fresh start. As Fr Timothy Radcliffe writes:

We are not the perfect parents, or the amazing spouses, or the spotless pious priests that we all may have imagined. But God smiles on us as we are, warts and all. We may not be perfect but neither are we despicable worms. We are fallible human beings who make our way to the kingdom, keeling over from time to time.

TIMOTHY RADCLIFFE, STATIONS OF THE CROSS
(LONDON: BLOOMSBURY, 2015), 22

What is important is that we get up and try again. And there is no limit to the number of times we can start afresh and try again. When Peter asks Jesus how many times he must forgive someone, "As many as seven times?" Jesus replies, "Not seven times, but, I tell you, seventy-seven times" (Matthew 18:21-22). We are all called to sainthood, chosen for a particular purpose, but it is a choice whether to take the path taken by Lucy, or by Edmund, or not to go through the wardrobe door at all.

The Lord will fulfil his purpose for me

PSALM 138:8A

It is in loving relationships that we find ourselves. We are who we are because of our relationships. In the Parable of the Mustard Seed in St Mark's Gospel, there is an idea that our relationship with Jesus is growing and developing even while we are sleeping. The seed grows by itself. This is our natural curiosity and longing for God. As it states in the Catechism of the Catholic Church, "The desire for God is written in the human heart, because man is created by God and for God; and God never ceases to draw man to himself. Only in God will he find the truth and happiness he never stops searching for" (*Catechism of the Catholic Church*, 27). St Augustine summed this up when he said, "you have made us for yourself, and our heart is restless until it rests in you". The Parable of the Mustard Seed tells us that from very small seeds, enormous faith can grow. The mustard seed is one of the smallest seeds, but it grows into one of the largest plants. Think about what would happen if a tiny mustard seed was planted in good soil where it could get all the water and sun it needed. This is what our faith – our relationship with God - is like. It may start small, it may stay small for a while, but if we give our faith what it needs, it grows and grows and becomes strong enough to get us through anything.

I've talked in Chapter Two about the need to recognise Jesus in order to discover who we truly are. How do we enter a relationship with Jesus? How do we try to become more like him? For Catholics, one of the ways of trying to achieve this is through the sacraments, and the Eucharist in particular. It is from Chapter Six of St John's Gospel that we gain much of our understanding of the Eucharist, and the Real Presence of Christ in the Eucharist:

I am the living bread that came down from heaven. Whoever eats of this bread will live for ever; and the bread that I will give for the life of the world is my flesh. For my flesh is true food, and my blood is true drink.

JOHN 6:51-55

It is worth meditating on this statement: "I am the living bread that came down from heaven". What does it say to you? That Jesus is what you need to be sustained? But he isn't just the bread of life, he is the *living bread*. If you look up "living" in the dictionary, you find definitions such as "an income sufficient to live on" and "the pursuit of a particular lifestyle". As an adjective, "living" means to be alive. So, Jesus is our spiritual means of support and nourishment, and he is also our way of life and, since he is living bread, he is alive in us. St Augustine said at the time of his conversion, "It was as though I heard a voice from on high: I am the food of the strong; eat then of me and grow. But you will not transform me into yourself like food for the body, but rather you will be transformed into me." (St Augustine *The Trumpet Shall Sound – The End of The World*, Chapter 26:2) Indeed, Pope Leo the Great said that "Our sharing in the Body and Blood of Christ has no other purpose than to transform us into that which we receive". This is perhaps the meaning of the living bread. Fr Jim McManus has written about how truly to become the Eucharist we celebrate. He challenges us to reflect on: "How will this impact on my life?" "What will it do to my relationships with others?" Our relationships with "others" includes Jesus.

In the Sermon on the Mount Jesus says we should all look at ourselves and our relationships with each other (and with God):

So when you are offering your gift at the altar, if you remember that your brother or sister has something against you, leave your gift there before the altar and go; first be reconciled to your brother or sister, and then come and offer your gift.

MATTHEW 5:23-24

The gift here is probably an offering brought to atone for a wrong done to another person. But this doesn't count if the wrong isn't first put right. One of the great prayers that understands the deep connection between self-awareness and God-awareness is from St Augustine: "Grant Lord, that I may know myself that I may know thee. Amen".

This book was written under the working title of *To Thine own Self be True*. Which is a line taken from Shakespeare's *Hamlet*. It is a line that my mother wrote in the birthday card she gave me on my eighteenth birthday. At the end of Act One Scene Three, Polonius says to his own son:

This above all: to thine own self be true,
And it must follow, as the night the day,
Thou canst not then be false to any man.
Farewell, my blessing season this in thee.

SHAKESPEARE *HAMLET*,
ACT ONE, SCENE THREE, LINES 79-82

Many parents have quoted from Polonius and given their children this advice. I always understood being true to myself as meaning that I should act in line with my own conscience, and only get involved with what I was comfortable with, though was right, and could live with. Literary scholars say that in the Elizabethan era words like "self" and "true" had a different meaning from today. Polonius' words may have had several meanings. Interestingly, in terms of this chapter, interpretations of these lines are similar to the Eurythmics song from which this chapter takes its inspiration. The first interpretation of this quotation from *Hamlet* chimes with my own; that we should always do the right thing and be honest in our actions and relationships. There is an idea here that we can judge ourselves better if we have done what we could and should have done. But there is also a view that by "true" Polonius meant beneficial, a number of scholars would argue that his advice to his son was to put himself and what was of benefit to him first. This is, I suppose, like telling our children to look after themselves. Perhaps Polonius meant for Laertes to put his own needs before others, but I would argue that really to look after yourself, and to live a life which is to your own beneficial interest, you need to put others first. It is treasure in heaven, rather than on earth, that we need to store up for ourselves.

If we are going to be true to ourselves in the sense of trying to do the right thing and follow the path laid down for us, then self-awareness is important. How well do you know yourself? Do you know what motivates you? Being self-aware means having a clear understanding of who we are, including our strengths and weaknesses, thoughts, beliefs, motivations and emotions. St Paul thought that he knew himself and that he was following his vocation when he was persecuting Christians. We need to have the awareness to question what we know about ourselves. This means developing a habit of self-reflection so that we can take some time to think about what is going on in our lives and what is really important. It also means inviting the opinions of those we trust about how they see us. It means thinking about how God sees us, and then, having taken stock, perhaps shifting our focus so that we reflect ourselves more truthfully.

Do not forsake the work of your hands
Psalm 138:8b

St Paul believed in his vocation and was motivated by his commitment to God. He initially set off down the wrong path, but God didn't turn away from Paul. God went and found Paul on the road to Damascus, and set him straight. Paul's vocation was now made perfectly clear to him, and his drive to serve God meant that he embraced this. God will not forsake us, even when we get things wrong. And it really is our choice whether to follow Christ. When Mary appeared to Bernadette at the grotto in Lourdes, she asked Bernadette, "Would you do me the kindness of coming here for fifteen days?" This was an invitation which recognised Bernadette's humanity. Made, as we are, in the image and likeness of God, we are all worthy of dignity and love. Bernadette was chosen by God for a particular purpose. She, like Mary before her, didn't have to say "yes".

Mary is a very special woman whom God chose to be the mother of Jesus. But God didn't choose Mary for her education, wealth or respectability (she wasn't married when she conceived Jesus). God took an ordinary woman and gave her an extraordinary opportunity. God has a definite purpose for who we should be and what we can do. But God won't make us do anything. When the angel Gabriel revealed God's plan for her, Mary could have said, "No, thank you." George Steiner talks about pictures which "speak", using Lorenzo Lotto's *Annunciation* as an example. When I first saw this painting, it really did speak to me, conveying the incredible emotion Mary must have felt. In this painting, Mary appears to turn her back on God. It is a fascinating piece that speaks to me of Mary's response to the angel Gabriel's news. There she is at home, going about her daily activities, when an angel suddenly appears to ask her to be the mother of God. Italian art critic Giulio Argan writes: "She cannot even turn her head; her gesture, almost a defensive one, is that of somebody who is struck at the back by a sudden call." St Luke writes that Mary was "much perplexed" by what the angel Gabriel said to her (Luke 1:29). Synonyms for "perplexed" include: confused, stunned, bewildered and thrown. Mary is perhaps recoiling from the angel. She's reeling: what will people think? I'm not married. What's going to happen to me now? How can this be happening? Can I handle this? We all fear what other people think of us, none of us likes criticism. We fear uncertainty and change. We experience feelings of inadequacy, and there are times when we can feel that too much is being asked of us. Mary felt all of this. When I look at Lotto's painting, I also imagine the next scene that he didn't paint. The scene where Mary turns back towards the angel Gabriel and says the words that will become part of the prayer, the *Magnificat*, "Let it be with me according to your word" (Luke 1:38).

I have talked about the lyrics of lots of psalms and songs throughout this book. Luke 1:46-55 is Mary's song. She praises God for what is happening in her life. Her song reveals her understanding of the psalms. Isn't it wonderful to think that all those years ago, Mary reflected on the same Book of Psalms as we do today? The question for us is, can we, like Mary, take a deep breath and turn and face God? How can we live out Mary's song spiritually?

He has scattered the proud in the thoughts of their hearts.
He has brought down the powerful from their thrones,
and lifted up the lowly;
he has filled the hungry with good things, and sent the
rich away empty.

LUKE 1:51-53

As the word of God becomes more deeply ingrained in us, it shapes our response to everything. Can we become like Mary, and let the word of God become part of our way of thinking and living? Are we proud or are we humble? Do we share our material and spiritual wealth with others?

Being diagnosed with a chronic illness is frightening, and it can feel that our lives have been really messed up. The pain and stress can be challenging. It is easy to become depressed, and to strike out at the people closest to us. But what is important is to know that chronic illness isn't a punishment from God. I know I haven't done anything to deserve MS. None of us have done anything to deserve the challenges that we face, and all of us are loved. I don't know how MS fits into God's plan for me. I don't believe God wants me to suffer. What I do know is that my MS has led me down a different path from the one I would have chosen myself. I also know that actually, I am now happy on the path I am travelling. And I know that I am not on my own and that I am part of something bigger. As President Jimmy Carter said:

I have one life and one chance to make it count for something . . . I'm free to choose what that something is, and the something I've chosen is my faith. Now, my faith goes beyond theology and religion and requires considerable work and effort. My faith demands - this is not optional - my faith demands that I do whatever I can, wherever I am, whenever I can, for as long as I can with whatever I have to try to make a difference.

I'll end this chapter with that quotation from Jimmy Carter, and some very similar words from scripture:

You are the light of the world. A city built on a hill cannot be hidden. No one after lighting a lamp puts it under the bushel basket, but on the lampstand, and it gives light to all in the house. In the same way, let your light shine before others, so that they may see your good works and give glory to your Father in heaven.

MATTHEW 5:14-16

We all crave the peace that only God can give.

Chapter Seven

God makes us a promise

The Lord is my shepherd, I shall not want.
He makes me lie down in green pastures;
he leads me beside still waters; he restores my soul.
He leads me in right paths for his name's sake.

Even though I walk through the darkest valley, I fear no evil;
for you are with me; and your rod and your staff – they comfort me.

You prepare a table before me in the presence of my enemies;
you anoint my head with oil; my cup overflows.
Surely goodness and mercy shall follow me all the days of my life,
and I shall dwell in the house of the Lord my whole life long.

PSALM 23

Pat Monahan, lead singer of Rock band Train, wrote *Drops of Jupiter (Tell Me)* after his mother died from lung cancer. The band had released their first album in 1998 and were touring while Pat's mum was dying. Pat made numerous stops during the tour to speak to his mum using pay phones, this was in the days before the widespread use of mobile phones. She died in the December of 1998. In his song, Pat wonders how his relationship with his mother has changed now that she has died – does she miss him? Does she miss the things she used to enjoy? Or, is her new existence too mind blowing to be bothered with earthly things? The song was an international hit, and won a Grammy award.

There was a song we used to sing when I was in the Brownies:

Oh you'll never get to heaven

In a baked bean tin

Because a baked bean tin

Has got baked beans in.

Of course, getting to heaven is actually, in some ways, the easy bit. We don't need a vehicle, baked bean tin or otherwise. Christ told us how we could get there: we need to love one another and serve one another. A friend of mine recently had a health scare. As he lay awake late one night, contemplating his mortality, he began to wonder if he wouldn't rather go to purgatory than heaven. "In purgatory you still have a choice," he said to me. "Once you're in heaven, that's it. You are there for eternity in a state of bliss. I want my free will!" When I was teaching secondary school RE, lessons about evil and suffering led onto discussion about the issue of free will. Often pupils couldn't understand why God allowed terrible things to happen, why he allowed suffering. This is something that is hard for us all to understand. But it is worth thinking about the fact that if the full spectrum of emotions and experiences were not available to us, and God stepped in to prevent us experiencing any suffering, we would live our lives in a state of anaesthesia. Perhaps this is a little how my friend fears heaven will be. Is there much difference between being in an enforced state of happiness for all eternity, and being anaesthetised, in the sense that all other emotions and experiences are shut off? Will we have a consciousness of our previous experiences and emotions after we have died? In life it can be difficult to remember how we felt about an experience once it has passed. The most obvious example is the pain of childbirth, which women often forget, only to be reminded when they are in the throes of giving birth to a subsequent child. Eternity is an unfathomably long time! What chance of remembering who we were or how we felt during our life on earth? Of course, there are some experiences we would perhaps like to forget. There is pain and unhappiness we would like relief from. We all crave the peace that only God can give.

It is impossible for any of us to know what heaven will be like. I remember as a child my then Parish Priest giving a particular homily at a school Mass. It was about a comment a six-year-old had made to him, "Wouldn't it be nice if we could take a bus to heaven for the day?" "Yes," he had replied to her, "but the problem is that heaven is such a wonderful place, no-one would want to come home again". Faith is about trust. We trust that God knows us better than we know ourselves. Human, earthly concepts about independence, boredom and continuing to have an enquiring mind are just that; earthly concepts. Once we have taken our one-way ticket to heaven, we trust we really will be in paradise. In the meantime, we can only wonder what that will be like.

"Tell me," demands Pat Monahan of his mum in his song, Where are you? What have you seen? And are you missing me? (Pat Monahan, *Drops of Jupiter* (*Tell Me*) (2001). Death changes our relationships, but it doesn't end them. The love we feel for the people we have lost doesn't die, it carries on. Although his physical relationship with his mother changed, Pat didn't stop being a son when his mother died. His mother's death signals a change in their relationship. Both have a new existence that they cannot share with one another. Pat's life changed, but as he sings in his song, his mum's death reminds him that that there is "time to change" and "room to grow".

The Lord is my shepherd, I shall not want

PSALM 23:1

The emotional bond with those we have lost can continue after their death, particularly if those we love die well. It's worth exploring here the theme of death and dying well. Death has become more remote from people's lives. I've never seen a dead body. We are also less used to people dying young. In the 1950s most deaths happened at home, today people mostly die in hospitals. But what makes a good death is having a good life. Surgeon and writer Attal Gwande reflects on the way we treat the very old and those who are dying, in his book *Being Mortal: Illness, Medicine and What Matters in the End* (London: Profile Books, 2014). Most people would rather be at home when they die, than in a hospital, so what has happened since the 1950s to reverse this trend? Attal Gawande says as economies improve, they hospitalise people at the end of their life rather than caring for them at home. It is, he has said, the result of "a mutual selfishness":

As soon as we had the economic means, as we got older we didn't want to live with the kids and have them taking care of us either, because we had to be under their rules, and no-one wanted that... it's not a cult of the young, it's a cult of the independent self, and then when you are no longer able fully to care for yourself, we put you in institutions, in old age homes or in hospitals, and there we say, you know what is most important, your safety and your health. Instead of understanding that people have priorities much larger than that. Priorities besides being safe and living longer no matter what.

ATAL GAWANDE SPEAKING ON *START THE WEEK*,
BBC RADIO 4, 10 NOVEMBER 2014

People want to have a purpose and know that they are doing more than just existing. This is interesting; part of what makes us who we are is a sense of purpose. As Attal explained to Andrew Marr, "People have things that they live for that are bigger than themselves, they may be as simple as a pet or a family, it may be as complex as wanting to contribute to a political debate, or write a book…or to be devoted to God. People need a bigger cause." Dying well is about dying with integrity and living out our final days with respect and our values intact. It is about approaching death as a natural process which is part of life, rather than with anxiety, fear and as a failure of medicine. The idea that the only good life is a healthy and independent one, misses the point that we all have the potential, even as our bodies decline, to live a good life. If comfort and acceptance can replace fear and anxiety, relationships have the opportunity to deepen in these final days. We can also make the choice to continue to be in a relationship with those we love after they have died.

Two years ago, my uncle died suddenly. I am still his niece. I keep in touch with his wife and my cousins, and take any opportunities I can to care for the people and causes he cared about. I try to maintain the values he cherished, one of which was spending time together as a family. This is a way of linking me to him, and it maintains his presence in my life. Speaking about writing *Drops of Jupiter (Tell Me)*, Pat Monahan has explained that the "loss of the most important person in my life was heavy on my mind, and [so was] the thought of what if no-one ever really leaves? What if she's here but different?" Pat's idea was that his mother was back in the atmosphere. This idea of never really leaving, and being here but different, is reminiscent of the Christian reality of the Resurrection. Mary Magdalene struggled to believe it was her good friend standing in front of her, when she met Jesus on Easter morning in the garden near the tomb where his body had been laid. Jesus was the same, but different. Mary doesn't recognise him immediately. When Mary realises it is Jesus, she reaches out, but is told by Jesus not to "hold on" to him. There is work to be done. She must go and tell the disciples Jesus is risen (John 20:1-2, 11-19). What has happened, has happened. It is time to look to the future. Our future is the hope of the promise of eternal life.

Christians believe in the resurrection of the body. St Paul writes in his letter to the Romans:

But if Christ is in you, though the body is dead because of sin, the Spirit is life because of righteousness. If the Spirit of him who raised Jesus from the dead dwells in you, he who raised Christ from the dead will give life to your mortal bodies also through his Spirit that dwells in you.

ROMANS 8:10-11

St Paul teaches that our bodies will also be changed and glorified after our death, "He will transform the body of our humiliation that it may be conformed to the body of his glory, by the power that also enables him to make all things subject to himself" (Philippians 3:21). Jesus' glorified body can't have looked exactly the same, because otherwise wouldn't Mary Magdalene have recognised him more quickly? And what about the disciples on the road to Emmaus and on the Sea of Tiberias? It doesn't make sense to say that they didn't recognise Jesus because they weren't expecting to see him, how often have we briefly mistaken a similar looking stranger on the other side of the road, for a loved one we know can't possibly be there? Jesus' glorified body is somehow different after his Resurrection. He has an agility which means he can appear and disappear at will, and doesn't need to use the door to enter a room. This is not something Jesus did before the Resurrection. In St Paul's letter to the Philippians, he writes that our lowly bodies will be improved. Any weakness, disease or other imperfection will be transformed to reflect the resurrected body of Jesus. This teaching underlines the point that we are more than our physical selves - a changed body does not mean a changed identity – but our bodies are an important part of our identity. Our bodies shape our identity, and our identity is intricately linked with the body we were born into.

He leads me in the right paths for his name's sake

PSALM 23:3

We live in an age which is fascinated by identity and by the body. This is highlighted particularly by current debates about gender identity. Understanding who we are is an important human need. I have prints of the children's hands and feet as babies, and I remember watching them exploring and learning about their own bodies – playing with their fingers and toes and holding them up to their faces to take a closer look, sucking them to see how they felt. It was as though they were trying to work out what their hands and feet were, and who they belonged to. In her book *Bodies* (London: Profile Books, 2010), Susie Orbach talks about the relationship between the body and the self in Western culture, and how this has changed over time. Before the Industrial Revolution, our bodies were our tool which we used to produce things. Farmers planted and grew crops, craftsmen manipulated materials to create objects. But in modern, Western society, Susie writes, "Our bodies are and have become a form of work. The body is turning from being the means of production to the production itself" (Susie Orbach, *Bodies* (London: Profile Books, 2010), 6. The body image which is held up as a modern ideal is lean, muscular and tanned. This would have once been the body of a working class labourer, whose body would look this way as a result of his physical labour. In history, as well as in less developed nations today, a lean, muscular and tanned body symbolises a lack of wealth as the poor generally have to work outdoors. In Western countries this "perfect" body image says something different. The opposite in fact, it says that people have the time and money to work on their body. A lean, muscular and tanned body is a privilege. But why such an obsessive interest in the body? Why do our bodies matter so much? Sarah Coakley writes:

In the late-twentieth-century affluent West, "the body", to be sure, is sexually affirmed, but also puritanically punished in matters of diet or exercise; continually stuffed with consumerist goods, but guiltily denied particular foods in aid of the "salvation" of a longer life; taught that there is nothing *but* it (the "body"), and yet asked to discipline it with an "I" that still refuses complete materialistic reduction.

SARAH COAKLEY, *POWERS AND SUBMISSIONS: SPIRITUALITY, PHILOSOPHY AND GENDER* (LONDON: BLACKWELL PUBLISHERS, 2002), 155

This quest for longevity, beauty, health and sexual performance, says Sarah Coakley, is a denial of death. But our death is something that we all need to spend some time thinking about. Sarah's writing also highlights another issue about our understanding of who we are. Our treatment of our bodies as noted here, raises the question of whether we see ourselves as separate from our bodies. Our bodies must make up part of who we are, because this identity is preserved when we are given back our own (glorified) body after we have died.

If I had met Sheila thirteen years ago, and she had said to me that my MS was a part of me – to be embraced – I would have been horrified. As horrified as Mo Mowlam was, in Neil McKay's screenplay, to consider the idea that her brain tumour had played a part in making her who she was. I had experienced changes in my handwriting, a temporary (but complete) loss of vision in my left eye, which was followed, as my sight slowly recovered, by the same in the right. Then there was the fatigue, numbness, double vision, shooting pains, a lack of balance and co-ordination and headaches. All of this felt like an attack on my person. But it wasn't being caused by an external force, it was coming from within me. Which I think is when I developed a dualistic idea about myself, and separated me from my body, I saw my body as a lesser, weaker, or even malevolent part of me, and sought to control it, ignoring symptoms in the hope I could overcome the MS. This allowed me to feel contempt for my MS. That is something that horrifies me now. In the months since I met Sheila, and have thought about our conversation, I can see more and more clearly why she reacted to me as she did. I had thought my attitude to my MS a healthy one. I got on with my life as before, it wouldn't beat me. But it is part of me, and can't be ignored. It is important not to curl up in a corner and give up, and I was right not to do that, but I should have worked at embracing my MS, embracing myself, sooner, instead of trying to ignore it. I'd fallen into Francis Bacon's way of thinking that it was possible to have power over nature.

Bacon was an English Philosopher who lived between 1561 and 1626. His ideas led to an understanding of nature as a mechanism. Pope St John Paul II believed that Bacon's thinking was the beginning of the split between the person and the body. Descartes also saw mind and body as two distinct substances, with the mind containing the soul as well as being the substance that thinks. These were ideas which St John Paul II tried to reconcile through his Theology of the Body, his teaching about the human person. John Paul wrote in his *Letter to Families* in 1984 "It is typical of rationalism to make a radical contrast in man between spirit and body, between body and spirit. But man is a person in the unity of his own body and his spirit. The body can never be reduced to mere matter." My doctors had never challenged me on my approach to my MS. The medics seemed to think it a healthy attitude. And so did I, but I don't think I do any more. My body is not a plane that I can pilot, I am not distinct from it. But it won't always be like this either. Gregory of Nyssa taught that our bodies are longing for transformation into the divine. He believed this process starts during our lives, and has its final goal in the future, after our death. It is interesting to look at Gregory's teaching to consider the question of how our identities (bodies) might be changed by our own death.

Gregory of Nyssa's teaching is interesting in terms of modern debates about gender and sexuality. Gregory believed that gender is disposed of, as our glorified body is transformed into a de-genitalised status similar to that of the angels. Our gender and sexuality has a significant impact on how our identities are shaped. This is part of what makes us human. What happens after death remains a mystery to us, but Gregory's ideas are thought-provoking, particularly when we look at gender in the Godhead. As the Catechism of the Catholic Church puts it, "God transcends the human distinction between the sexes. He is neither man nor woman; he is God" (*Catechism of the Catholic Church*, 239). The Church of England's transformation steering group made headlines in 2015, when it began talking about whether the language used in their church services could be made more inclusive. WATCH (Women and the Church) started a conversation about God and gender. There is talk of God's motherly love in the Bible, both Matthew and Luke quote Jesus in identical words: "Jerusalem, Jerusalem, the city that kills the prophets and stones those who are sent to it! How often have I desired to gather your children together as a hen gathers her brood under her wings, and you were not willing!" (Matthew 23:37 and Luke 13:34). We can only struggle to describe God in terms of what we know. I pray to "God the Father", and since I have had my own children, I now understand God more deeply as a parent. But I also understand God as a loving force, a creative energy, and experience God in the beauty and power of creation. In Isaiah we are given the example of an infant at its mother's breast as an image of God's loving care for us: "Can a woman forget her nursing child, or show no compassion for the child of her womb? Even these may forget, yet I will not forget you" (Isaiah 49:15). Just as the medieval mystic, Julian of Norwich, said: "As truly as God is our Father, so truly God is our Mother." This is a wonderful notion which is beautifully represented in Rembrandt's *The Return of the Prodigal Son*. In this painting, inspired by the Parable of the Prodigal Son, the father is depicted with two hands embracing his son – one is a larger, more muscular, male hand, and the other a smaller, feminine hand.

Stephen Bullivant has addressed the issue of gender in the Godhead in his book *The Trinity: How Not to Be a Heretic* (Boston: Pauline Press, 2015). He discusses the ideas of a number of Early Church teachers, including St Jerome, who mentions in his Commentary on Isaiah that the non-canonical Gospel of the Hebrews refers to "my mother, the Holy Spirit". Bullivant quotes St Jerome, "No one ought to be scandalised in this matter because in Hebrew the Spirit is spoken of in the feminine gender, when in [Latin] the masculine gender is applied, and in Greek the neuter; for in the Godhead, there is no gender (*in divinitate enim nullus est sexus*)." I wonder if you can flip this, and say, all gender is represented in the Godhead, given we are made in the image and likeness of God?

Even though I walk through the darkest valley, I fear no evil

PSALM 23:4

Death affects all aspects of life, touching our emotions and influencing our identity. As well as the question of how our own death may alter our identity as we are transformed in the divine, there is also the question of what happens to our identity after a death while on earth. When Muhammad Ali died in June 2016, George Foreman spoke of "losing a piece" of himself. Ali's death left Foreman as the only living boxer from the "golden age" of heavyweights like Joe Frazier, Jimmy Young, Ron Lyle, Ken Norton and Jimmy Ellis. "Each time one of us leaves, I tell everybody: Muhammad Ali, Joe Frazier, George Foreman, we were all just really one guy. And every time one slips away, you feel like you've lost a piece, and Muhammad Ali was the greatest piece of all" (Jessica Elgot, "Louisville to pay tribute to Muhammad Ali in street procession", *The Guardian*, 5 June 2016). We define ourselves through others and when people die we can feel as though we lose a part of ourselves. We can't look at our friends and loved ones any more to see ourselves, reflected in their perception. Identity is about relationship. Look at the difference in the disciples at the Last Supper, as compared with fifty days later, huddled together in a locked room, waiting for the Holy Spirit. And then, full of confidence, once they had the Spirit with them. In Christian understanding, the starting point for identity is that all humans are made in the image of a Trinitarian God. The Catechism of the Catholic Church teaches that, "by sending his only Son and the Spirit of Love in the fullness of time, God has revealed his innermost secret: God himself is an eternal exchange of love, Father, Son and Holy Spirit, and he has destined us to share in that exchange" (*Catechism of the Catholic Church*, 221). We too, therefore, are an eternal exchange of love. It is interesting that neuroscience confirms this to some extent.

Children's experiences in their earliest years affect how their brains work, the way they respond to stress, and their ability to form trusting relationships. It is during these early years that the brain undergoes its most dramatic growth, setting the stage for social and emotional development. The back-and-forth interactions of babies and adults shape a baby's brain architecture, supporting the development of communication and social skills. All aspects of child development are interconnected: emotional, cognitive, social and physical development are interrelated and influence each other. To be human is to need others. Our first experience of life is close contact with another. We can hear our mother's heartbeat in the womb, and after birth we like to be (and generally are) held closely. Research has shown that even very premature babies, born between twenty-eight and thirty-one weeks, benefit from human touch. Among other benefits, skin to skin contact can reduce the stress response. Touch is the first sense we acquire and is vital to successful relationships, including our relationship with God, who reaches out and touches us through the sacraments. The laying on of hands is a significant part of the sacrament of ordination, which also involves anointing the palms. Baptism and confirmation also involve touch, as does the sacrament of the sick.

The sacrament of the sick recognises a person's full human integrity. Doctors care for the body; they treat an illness. The sacrament of the sick is about giving care and dignity to the whole person. Touch is an important part of this sacrament. In the past oil was placed on the eyes, ears, nostrils, lips and hands - the parts of the body relating to five senses - as well as the feet and sometimes in the case of men, the loins. Since 1972 a simplified version of the sacrament has been given; now usually only the hands and forehead are anointed with olive oil. My parish priest has preached about this sacrament, making two observations that struck me in particular: the medicalisation of death, and the importance of touch. I have little experience of caring for someone who is dying, but I identified powerfully with what he said, because of my experience of giving birth. Here again the medical profession is often heavily involved, and again in rather a confused way. Just as death is difficult for doctors because it implies failure, birth poses difficulties because it is also a natural process and not an illness. It was late in the evening by the time I was moved onto a ward after Edgar's birth; and my mum and husband had to go home. It hadn't been an easy birth experience and I remember feeling I needed to hold onto someone, and asking my midwife if I could just hold her hand for a few minutes. She obliged. At other times all public sector workers can do is respond to others with touch. During the inquest held into the 7/7 bombings in London in 2005, there was a moving account by one of the fire fighters, who was with a twenty-one-year-old man in the underground before he died, "I felt for a pulse and we made eye contact, and there was still some life there. It was still there, it didn't last long but it was still there. I gave him a cuddle" ("7/7 inquiry: I felt for a pulse. There was still life. It didn't last. I cuddled him", *The Scotsman*, 1 November 2010). Touching someone recognises their humanity. On 27 August 2016 more than two hundred and fifty people were killed in a massive earthquake in central Italy.

Rescuers used their bare hands to search for survivors trapped by collapsed buildings. This was a powerful example of the use of touch to save lives, as is the action of eight-year-old Giulia Rinaldo, who gave her own life by throwing herself on top of her four-year-old sister, Georgia, when the ceiling of their home collapsed. A firefighter left a note on her coffin, apologising for getting to her too late to save her: "Ciao, little one, I gave a hand trying to pull you out of the prison of rubble. Sorry we didn't make it in time" (Nick Squires and Henry Samuel, "'Ciao, little one. Sorry we didn't make it in time': Italy mourns earthquake dead at mass funeral", *The Telegraph*, 27 August 2016).

Jesus heals people using touch throughout his ministry. There are numerous accounts in the Gospels of Christ touching people when he healed or blessed them: when a leper came to him Jesus stretched out his hand and touched him (Mark 1:41-43); Jesus felt the power leave him as a woman (believing Jesus could heal her) touched his cloak as he passed (Luke 8:47-48); he touches and heals a man who has been blind from birth (John 9:1-17).

Mary Magdalene's response at seeing Jesus after his resurrection is to reach out and touch him. The physicality of the risen Jesus assures us that death is not the end. It does seem odd that Jesus tells Mary not to touch him, later he will invite Thomas the Twin to put his hand in his side. The Latin *Noli me tangere*, which means "don't touch me", was originally written in Greek, and perhaps might be better translated as "cease holding on to me" or "stop clinging to me". This might imply that Mary is already touching Jesus, hugging him maybe. Is it possible that the problem is not that Mary couldn't or shouldn't touch Jesus, or that this was in some way wrong, but rather that there are other priorities; like him going to his Father, and her going to tell the disciples he is risen? We are told in the same Gospel account that describes Mary's encounter with the risen Christ, that Thomas refused to believe Jesus had risen from the dead, "Unless I see the mark of the nails in his hands, and put my finger in the mark of the nails and my hand in his side" (John 20:24). Jesus later comes to Thomas, "Put your finger here and see my hands. Reach out your hand and put it in my side. Do not doubt but believe" (John 20:27). Here touch is used to prove both Christ's humanity and his divinity. Jesus' physical human person has been resurrected by his Father, he has been glorified.

But why didn't Mary and the other disciples recognise Jesus straight away? What will our glorified bodies look like and will we be recognisable to those we love? Mary's failure to recognise Jesus worries some people, who fear they will fail to recognise and be recognised by their loved ones after they have died. Why did Mary have trouble recognising Jesus when he appeared to her after the Resurrection? Luke recounts the story of the two disciples on the road to Emmaus, who fail to recognise Jesus until he breaks bread with them (24:13-35). In this account Luke explains why the disciples don't immediately recognise Jesus, "While they were talking and discussing, Jesus himself came near and went with them, but their eyes were kept from recognising him" (24:15). This is an interesting account. Were the disciple's eyes kept from recognising Jesus supernaturally, so that Jesus could teach them how the Old Testament prophecies about the Messiah were fulfilled by him, without them becoming over-excited and not listening attentively to this teaching? Or, was it their human grief and despondency that stopped them from seeing who was walking with them. We are told in Luke's account that they looked sad (24:17). You can imagine them walking along the road, barely looking up, wrapped up in their thoughts and feelings, deep in conversation, grief-stricken, bereft. Whether it was as a result of a force outside of themselves, or their own grief and preoccupation, these disciples didn't see who Jesus was until he took the bread, blessed and broke it, and gave it to them. This is interesting, and so is the conversation that happens between them immediately afterwards: "Then their eyes were opened, and they recognised him; and he vanished from their sight. They said to each other, 'Were not our hearts burning within us while he was talking to us on the road, while he was opening the scriptures to us?'" (24:32). The disciples recognise Jesus by his actions and the way they felt in his company. We are who we are because of the values we hold, and the things that we do, and others recognise when we are near because of the way they feel in our presence. The uncle of mine who died suddenly was the sort of person who lit up a room, the life and soul of the party. When he was near, people relaxed, and laughed. The last time I saw him he was telling a story about a squirrel. It was a story that I had heard before, but could never tire of hearing, it always made me laugh until tears were running down my cheeks. On that particular afternoon, I was busy with the children, and only heard part of the story being recounted as I put out the recycling. I can clearly recall wishing that I could stop and listen to the story again, but that there would be another time. None of Uncle Kenny's stories are as funny when told by anyone else. He was a master story teller, and it was his inability to get through a story without laughing uncontrollably, that probably made everyone else laugh. I won't need Kenny to look the same to be able to recognise him. I just need to hear the start of the story about the squirrel in the flat above the video shop in Camberley, and I'll be laughing so hard that the tears running down my cheeks will stop me being able to see him clearly anyway. I'll know it's him.

Surely goodness and mercy shall follow me all the days of my life

PSALM 23: 6

Is that what happened to Mary Magdalene in the garden on Easter morning? John tells us she was weeping (20:11). Did the tears in her eyes stop her from seeing Jesus' face clearly? She recognises him when he says her name, which is possibly the first time she has properly looked up. On the Sea of Tiberias, the disciples perhaps struggle to recognise Jesus immediately because it is just after daybreak and the boat is out at sea – about a hundred yards. Maybe they just can't see very well, because Thomas is able to identify Jesus – and his physical scars - immediately (John 20: 24-29). But again, when Jesus appears on the shore by the Sea of Tiberias, it is the exchange between Jesus and the disciples that tells Peter that "It is the Lord!" (21:6-7). It is by our actions and how we engage with others that we are recognised.

We are social beings. Atul Gawande wrote a piece in the *New Yorker* in 2009 about long-term isolation in US prisons, citing evidence of its ineffectiveness as well as its cruelty: "Human beings are social creatures," he said, "We are social not just in the trivial sense that we like company, and not just in the obvious sense that we each depend on others. We are social in a more elemental way: simply to exist as a normal human being requires interaction with other people." In which case, what makes us who we are, are those around us and our relationships with one another. So, rather than looking inwardly to discover our identities, we can only really understand who we are by looking outwards. Jesus says, "Those who find their life will lose it, and those who lose their life for my sake will find it" (Matthew 10:39). It is when we lose ourselves in service to others, and relationship with something bigger, that we find greater spirituality, happiness, and our true selves. This is something well understood by those with a terminal illness, or who are elderly, and perhaps to some extent by those of us living with conditions like MS. Speaking on BBC Radio 4's *Start the Week* programme on 10 November 2014, Atul Gawande told Andrew Marr that the elderly and terminally ill become, "less focused on acquisition and public achievement and those kinds of things, and become more focused on a tight, smaller, group of people with whom they want to have deeper, more intimate relationships, be connected to and have purpose expressed through these kinds of relationships." Christ has called us to help each other in bodily service. As St Teresa of Avila said, "Christ has no body on earth but yours, no hands but yours, yours are the eyes through which Christ's compassion is to look out to the earth, yours are the feet by which he is to go about doing good and yours are the hands by which he blesses us now." Reaching out to reassure and comfort each other is one way of answering that call, and in answering Christ's call we perhaps begin to walk along the path towards making our own flesh glorious. God's comfort is greater than our suffering.

...now I'm getting up and brushing off the dust. My vision is clearing.

God is faithful forever

Out of the depths I cry to you, O Lord.
Lord, hear my voice!
Let your ears be attentive to the voice of my supplications!

If you, O Lord, should mark iniquities, Lord, who could stand?
But there is forgiveness with you, so that you may be revered.

I wait for the Lord, my soul waits, and in his word I hope;
my soul waits for the Lord more than those who watch for the
morning, more than those who watch for the morning.

O Israel, hope in the Lord!
For with the Lord there is steadfast love, and with him is great power
to redeem.
It is he who will redeem Israel from all its iniquities.

PSALM 130

I've chosen Psalm 130 to end with, because this psalm is used in night prayer at the end of the day, and because I like the "roar" in it. Those first lines don't ask to be heard, they demand it. It is also notable and relevant that there is a shift from the singular and personal, to the plural and the whole nation of Israel.

Katy Perry wrote a song called *Roar* with Bonnie Leigh McKee, Henry Walter, Lukasz Gottwald and Max Martin. The song, which was released in 2013, begins with lyrics about being scared to rock the boat and accepting life's events passively, so passively that Katy sings she stood for nothing and fell for everything.

These are lyrics which sum up the way I felt about the process of my diagnosis. I was passive. My choices had been taken away. I couldn't rock the boat, because I was too scared for a little while even to move, and I had no idea which way to turn.

It was the prospect of children which gave me back some control over the situation I found myself in. The drug therapies offered to me were not suitable if I was pregnant or breast feeding, so I put off taking them. All medicines have side effects, and for as long as I am able, I would rather be drug free. I am one of many others living with a similar diagnosis, and I have been extraordinarily lucky so far: no motor symptoms, and, interestingly, since the birth of my eldest son, fewer sensory symptoms. Now I was making some decisions for myself again. I'd had a baby, and I didn't at this point want to try any medication. The second verse of *Roar* is playing in my head: now I'm getting up and brushing off the dust. My vision is clearing.

The fatigue can be difficult, there are other challenges, but I can function. I'm married with two young sons; I write freelance for the Church press; have authored a couple of education titles; I'm a qualified teacher with a PhD in Education; I edited the Mowbray Lent Book 2013; I work as administrator for my Parish Priest; and I am the Chair of Governors at the local Catholic Primary school. With the exception of my teaching qualification, all of this has been achieved since 2003. I'm active, and swim regularly. There are those who think I should do less. But I am grateful I can do as much as I do, and I will carry on and do what I can, in loving service, for as long as I can: I'm a fighter, I'm dancing "and you're gonna hear me roar!" (Katy Perry, Bonnie Leigh McKee, Henry Walter, Lukasz Gottwald and Max Martin, *Roar*, 2013).

This book is due to be published in my fortieth year. That's a pretty loud roar. Now it's time for some discernment about my own life and where I go next. Although that isn't a decision entirely for me, it is impacted by those around me. What does God want me to be? James and Edgar are growing up, and will be leaving home in another ten years. That's not long when I think about how quickly the first ten years in James' life seemed to pass. It's time to think about Pope Francis' questions: "Do we have great vision and impetus? Are we also daring? Do our dreams fly high?" Of course, there has to be a certain amount of realism in this thinking. I'm not going to be able to begin a new career and work a forty hour week, and I wouldn't want to. Within the pages of this book I have made the point about our lives and identity being about more than our employment or usefulness. Our lives are about vocation, and choosing whether or not we want to become the person God wants us to be.

There is a myth in society that we are self-sufficient and don't need anyone else; a view that to need others implies weakness. Perhaps needing others does make us weak, but if this is so then we are all weak - or vulnerable - and this is indeed a creative part of human living. We all need each other, even Jesus needed others. On his journey to the cross he has the support of his mother, Simon of Cyrene helps to carry his cross, and "Veronica" (which actually means "true image" and refers to the cloth rather than the woman) wipes his face. There are times we all need help and support. I am learning to embrace my MS and see it as a blessing and a positive transformative experience. It has taught me that I am not on my own. This in itself has been empowering to some extent. As St Paul writes in his letter to the Corinthians, "For whenever I am weak, then I am strong" (2 Corinthians 12:10).

I recall, years before my diagnosis, overhearing a conversation about someone who was ill, and how this person had "found God". The conversation was sympathetic, but insinuated that those who were ill turn to religion because their circumstances are difficult and this is their last vain refuge: "Poor thing, it's all she's got left". Ultimately, God is all that is left. But how wonderful that fact is. Jesus shared our weakness, now we can share his strength. I turned to God at the time of my diagnosis not because I felt hopeless, but because it is rude not to talk to someone standing right next to you, and Jesus was there, day and night, at my elbow. Talking to him was easy at that time. The thing about Jesus is that he has been there and done that. In the mystery of the Incarnation and in his passion and death, what we have in Jesus is, as Kevern writes, "the perfect expression of the self-emptying God" (Peter Kevern, "Sharing the mind of

Christ: preliminary thoughts on dementia and the Cross", *New Blackfriars*, 91 / 1034 (July 2010), 418. This idea of "self-emptying" of one's own will and becoming entirely receptive to God's, is known in Christian theology as kenosis. It comes from St Paul, who writes in his letter to the Philippians:

> *Let the same mind be in you that was in Christ Jesus, who, though he was in the form of God, did not regard equality with God as something to be exploited, but emptied himself, taking the form of a slave, being born in human likeness. And being found in human form, he humbled himself and became obedient to the point of death – even death on a cross.*

PHILIPPIANS 2:5-9

I have been given back my "roar", but now I am ready to give it away. Last time, I felt it had been taken from me. This time, I am willing to surrender it to God. God is love, and if I was writing any more after these pages, I would be talking about Shania Twain's *You're Still The One* as the inspiration:

> You're still the one I run to
> The one that I belong to
> You're still the one I want for life...

ROBERT JOHN LANGE AND
SHANIA TWAIN,
YOU'RE STILL THE ONE (1997)

Giving up my "roar" doesn't mean giving up. It means responding to Jesus' invitation and looking to find where he is pointing me.

I have come to the conclusion, in the process of writing this book, that our identity as we pass through life is fluid. The essence of who we are is held and retained by God, and the person we become is up to us. And here I mean "us" collectively. I come back to that wonderful line in Kathryn Greene-McCreight's book which I quoted at the beginning of the book: "The people of God is not just a collection of individuals, but a web of relationships created by God. We are not our own. We are not on our own" (Kathryn Greene-McCreight, *I Am With You* (London: Bloomsbury, 2015), 97-98.

St Paul teaches that we are one body, one spirit, in Christ. In the Godhead, there is one essence and three persons. What makes us who we are is the invitation to share and live in that essence, as the people we are. Who we are is all about relationship. The most important relationship I have is with God. Through this relationship, the rest of my relationships grow and develop, and it is these relationships which make me who I am. My MS has undoubtedly increased my faith, which in turn has developed who I am as a person. Our identity is not static. We are changed and shaped by those we meet and our relationship to them. My MS has helped to make me who I am not because of my condition exactly, but because of the relationships that have been sparked and developed because of my diagnosis. It is part of my story, and so Sheila is right, it is a part of me.